Praise for *glob•ali•zá•tion*

"This extremely well-written book explodes some of the myths about globalization. For those who want to better understand the economic issues raised by globalization, this book is a must read."

—Frederic S. Mishkin, Alfred Lerner
Professor of Banking and Financial Institutions,
Graduate School of Business, Columbia University,
former member of the Board of Governors of the Federal Reserve System,
author of *The Next Great Globalization:*
How Disadvantaged Nations Can Harness Their Financial Systems to Get Rich

"Bruce Greenwald and Judd Kahn masterfully demystify "globalization" and forcefully rebut the fears of job loss in the developed world as a result of trade. Bringing a popular Columbia Business School class to life, the book is a must-read for business people and commentators—and our new President."

—R. Glenn Hubbard, Dean and Russell L. Carson
Professor of Finance and Economics at Columbia Business School

"In their book on globalization, Greenwald and Kahn have done what seemed impossible. They have written a short, eminently readable book that explains the economics of globalization to the non-specialist. They dispel our ignorance, refute or refine the myths and cliches that dominate current public discourse, and show that globalization is an opportunity, not a threat. And they have managed to do all this with clear and lively prose, data that English majors can understand, and admirable balance and nuance."

—Peter H. Schuck, Simeon E. Baldwin
Professor at Yale Law School,
co-editor (with James Q. Wilson) of *Understanding America:*
The Anatomy of an Exceptional Nation (Public Affairs)

glob•ali•za´•tion

*The irrational fear that
someone in China
will take your job*

Bruce C. Greenwald
and Judd Kahn

WILEY

John Wiley & Sons, Inc.

Published by John Wiley & Sons, Inc., Hoboken, New Jersey.
Published simultaneously in Canada.

For general information on our other products and services or for technical support,
please contact our Customer Care Department within the United States at (800)
762-2974, outside the United States at (317) 572-3993 or fax (317) 572-4002.

Wiley also publishes its books in a variety of electronic formats. Some content
that appears in print may not be available in electronic books. For more
information about Wiley products, visit our web site at www.wiley.com.

Library of Congress Cataloging-in-Publication Data:

Greenwald, Bruce C. N., 1946-
    Globalization : the irrational fear that someone in China will take
your job / Bruce C. Greenwald, Judd Kahn.
      p. cm.
    Includes bibliographical references and index.
    ISBN 978-0-470-16963-6 (cloth)
      1. Globalization—Economic aspects. 2. International trade.
3. Labor market. 4. International economic relations. I. Kahn, Judd, 1940-
II. Title.
    HF1379.G744 2009
    337—dc22
                                   2008028064

Printed in the United States of America

10 9 8 7 6 5 4 3 2 1

*To Norbert W. Doyle, one of the great
unsung theorists of globalization,
and for Sara, Nora, Mateo, and Alessandro,
global grandchildren*

Contents

Acknowledgments

This book arose chiefly out of a course on globalization that Bruce has taught since 2002 with Joseph Stiglitz. It has benefited greatly from his kind and helpful comments, his broad knowledge of globalization, and his keen economic insight. It has also profited from the contributions of over 1,000 outstanding students who have taken the course and actively challenged and improved the material. Readers familiar with the literature on globalization will note the extent to which the positions taken here differ from those articulated by Professor Stiglitz's own first-rate books on the subject. Those differences are entirely our responsibility. He did his best to make us see the light as he sees it. The fact that both views coexist in the same course, and have been tolerated by the students, is testimony to the enduring value of civilized academic discourse. We are grateful to Professor Stiglitz and to the students.

We would also like to thank John Wright, the world's most supportive agent, Pamela van Giessen and Emilie Herman of John Wiley & Sons for their help and encouragement, and Ava Seave and Anne Rogin for everything.

Introduction

Just How Global Are We?

Globalization is a big deal. It envelops us, like the weather. To borrow the reactions of an early reader of this manuscript, "We sense it. We live it. We hear it in the voice on the phone. We see it in the closing of local shops and the opening of supermarkets with French names. We certainly experience it talking with the help desk, when the 800 number we called is clearly answered in some exotic place eight or ten time zones away from us." A nightly program on a major news channel is devoted to the perils of globalization. A search of Amazon.com for books with *globalization* in the title returns over 4,000 names, and the catalogue of the New York Public Library has almost 500 (with this book yet to be included).

But when we leave the indefinite *we* of this statement and coolly examine our own specific lives, these feelings look more like fantasy than fact. We (the authors) live in one of the great global cities (New York) and are affiliated with a great global university (Columbia). Yet in most of the things we do, we neither sense nor see nor experience lives substantially different from the ones we led before globalization permeated the atmosphere and the airwaves. The balance between foreign and domestic, global and local, exotic and familiar, has not been dramatically altered.

More students, especially doctoral candidates, come from overseas, but that trend has a long history. The flood of foreigners doesn't apply to education in general, not to elementary or high schools, not even to most colleges. Also, globalization implies a reciprocal relationship, and the number of American students going abroad for their education remains minuscule. There are more immigrants than 20 years ago, but the history of New York City is filled with successive waves of immigration, and the proportion of foreign-born residents is basically the same as it was in 1900 (36%), and lower than in 1910 (41%).

We live in typically American homes or apartments, send our children to typically American schools, shop for the most part in typically American stores, are treated by American certified (if not American-born) doctors in American hospitals, work largely with other Americans, and, with limited exceptions, eat American food. To be sure, many of the goods we buy are either made abroad or produced in the United States by foreign companies. But that is also an old story, dating back to at least the early 1980s, when all things Japanese represented the wave of the future. We have yet to see, but eagerly anticipate, the openings of local supermarkets with French names and French products. When local shops close, they are most frequently replaced by chains like Wal-Mart, Barnes & Noble, Home Depot,

Bed Bath & Beyond, Target, and in New York, Duane Reade—
all bona fide American companies. Foreign banks such as HSBC
have made an appearance, but when they do, they operate not
as foreign entities but under U.S. regulations and are scarcely
distinguishable from their American competitors, who continue
to dominate the market. The phone company remains thor-
oughly American. The principal novel element of globalization
in our experience is the occasional voice on the other end of
the phone from Cork or Mumbai. If that is truly the extent
of how the new globalization is penetrating our lives, it is a very
meager thing indeed. Globalization has a far larger presence in
the news than it does in our daily rounds, and as New Yorkers
our lives are probably more cosmopolitan than most.

To its critics, globalization is a terrible development that
makes almost everybody worse off and threatens the survival
of the planet. They blame it for everything from mass poverty in Africa and Latin America to the falling living standards
for workers in Europe and North America. They also charge
it with subverting local democracies, when powerful international corporations exert unchecked power in pursuit of their
own narrow self-interest. In contrast, globalization's advocates
argue that it is the greatest force for good in human history.
According to Martin Wolf, a well-informed and articulate pro-
ponent of globalization, and chief economics commentator for
the *Financial Times*,

> . . . a world integrated through the market should be
> highly beneficial to the vast majority of the world's
> inhabitants. The market is the most powerful institution
> for raising living standards ever invented. . . . The prob-
> lem today is not that there is too much globalization
> but that there is too little. (Wolf, *Why Globalization
> Works*, preface, xvii)[1]

Between these extremes, opinions range from generally positive but with warning signals about tough times ahead (Thomas Friedman, *The World Is Flat*), to generally negative but with a nod to potential benefits (Joseph Stiglitz, *Globalization and Its Discontents*).[2]

Despite the disagreements about its merits, a surprising consensus about the nature of globalization cuts across all these divergent views. There are five fundamental assumptions about globalization that are widely taken for granted:

1. Globalization is the future, an irresistible and growing part of economic reality.
2. Globalization is the dominant force shaping the world's economies. Whether for good or ill, whatever happens is due to globalization. Fixing the future means fixing globalization.
3. The fate of the world's workers depends on globalization, both in rich countries and in developing ones. Those who adapt will do well; those who do not will suffer.
4. Businesses face the same imperative. Either they globalize successfully or they stagnate and may even die.
5. Financial markets will be the most affected by globalization. Trying to resist the forces of financial globalization is like trying to turn back the tide.

The problem with these accepted truths is that they are either highly questionable or largely false. It is time to take a deep breath and look more closely at the real impact of this phenomenon as of today, and to assess its future in the same sober spirit.

Our goal in this book is to present a more accurate picture of the present status of globalization and its future consequences. A good place to begin is by understanding why the conventional wisdom is so wide of the mark and therefore provides such a shaky foundation for predicting the future of a global world.

First, most of the people writing on the subject treat globalization as something entirely novel. The process is rarely examined from a historical perspective detailed enough to distinguish something genuinely new from something that has occurred before in slightly different form. Some commentators, such as Thomas Friedman, paint historical comparisons with such a broad brush that they are of little use.

In the late 1950s and into the 1960s, as imports started to flood into the United States and ultimately exceeded exports, commentators worried about whether the United States was losing its competitive edge to other countries, especially the recovering economies in postwar Europe. By the 1970s and into the 1980s, it had become "Japan, Inc." that embodied the forces of global competition, which were going to undermine the economies of both Europe and the United States. In the early 1990s, Ross Perot heard a "giant sucking sound" that was supposed to record the rapid exit of jobs moving from the United States to a low-wage haven in Mexico.

None of these dire forecasts about the impending decline of the U.S. economy came to pass. If we can understand why they fell wide of the mark, we will be better positioned to anticipate the likely consequences of today's globalization bogeymen, the threats from China and India. Yet no one has seriously compared the current situation with these earlier episodes that have such a similar look and feel.

Second, by concentrating so intently on globalization, we ignore the role of other important trends and attribute every change to globalization. A similar misconception took place in England during the first half of the nineteenth century, during what may have been the earliest debates on international economic integration. There was a widespread fear, especially among landowners, that a flood of cheap food from North and South America, produced on recently opened acreage and using modern farming techniques, would bury British agriculture. Since few imagined that Britain could survive without its food-producing farms, the collapse of agriculture was widely regarded as the death knell of British prosperity. But powerful trends in productivity and consumption patterns were able to offset the impact of imported food. High productivity growth in agriculture, combined with limits on the demand for raw food and other agricultural commodities, were making agriculture a steadily diminishing part of overall British economic activity, even without the import of cheap foods. Today, farms in Britain are a quaint, expensive, and negligible part of a national economy that is many times larger than when concerns about agricultural decline were rampant.

People in Europe and America currently concerned about globalization focus on the loss of jobs in manufacturing and routine services, which they fear will be either imported from China or provided by a back office or call center in India. Yet improvements in productivity and changes in demand are doing to manufacturing and routine services what they did to agriculture in the nineteenth century—making them cheaper and therefore less central to the economy. Ignoring these powerful trends and other broad forces at work produces a distorted view of the impact and significance of globalization.

The third glaring weakness with the globalization debate is that it largely ignores information that is essential to understanding what is really going on. There are readily available data on occupation and employment, on the composition of national output and trade, on economic development and growth, on business profitability, and on the balance of payments and debt levels that, properly interpreted, could help resolve at least some of the disagreements. Instead, for much of the literature, the preferred form of evidence is the anecdote: the friend who finds himself competing with Indian data service providers, the radiologists who read American X-rays in Bangalore and transmit back the results, the bank data center in Manila. These stories command attention and elicit sympathy, but there is no way to tell whether they are interesting anomalies or telling examples of the wave of the future. Sometimes, as in the oft-cited case of the coming surge of Indian radiologists, who receive X-ray and other diagnostic files from U.S. hospitals and return interpretations of them over the same Internet connections, they turn out to be simply false.

Aware that anecdotes are not enough to make a solid case, some writers have buttressed their stories with references to academic studies that are based on systematic analyses of data. But a substantial number of these studies have fundamental flaws that simply get ignored in the summary references. For example, reports have claimed to show that under current global conditions, landlocked, mountainous countries never develop modern standards of living. Bolivia, Paraguay, Kazakhstan and all the "stans" of the former Soviet Union, Afghanistan, and Mongolia are offered up as examples, with Switzerland the only counterexample. But looked at more broadly, what we see is that large parts of Latin America and Central Asia have failed to develop coastal plains as well as remote highlands. Central Europe, however, and the states and provinces in the central United States and Canada, have succeeded. Properly considered, the underlying evidence on which these studies are based is at best inconclusive; at worst it tells a story quite different from the one that it is intended to support.

In a similar vein, these studies often treat each year's data as a separate and equally compelling piece of evidence. Yet year-to-year differences may be due to random, short-term fluctuations. This is "noise" and it can obscure important conclusions and allow spurious relationships to take their place. One frequently cited conclusion is that greater openness to trade—knocking down tariffs and other barriers to both imports and exports—is essential if any nation hopes to develop a modern standard of living. This finding is based on the parallel growth over time in a country's trade and in its gross domestic product, and it assumes that increasing trade makes the country more prosperous.

In fact, the causal relationship almost certainly runs the other way—greater prosperity leads to increased trade. Chinese and Indian exports began to swell in the 1980s and 1990s, not because these countries suddenly opened themselves to export markets, but because they had begun to eliminate the dead hand of oppressive domestic economic systems. These changes unleashed local economic energies, which led to rapid productivity growth and quality improvements. Only then did China and India have things to export that the rest of the world wanted, and at competitive prices. At the same time, rising incomes generated a demand for imports. The rise in measured international trade was clearly a result of these domestic reforms. Instead of trade leading to overall economic development, development drove trade.

One other tactic employed by writers on globalization is to quote from experts. But expert opinion is available on all sides of these issues, and writers on globalization, like everybody else, have a far higher estimate of the intelligence and expertise of those who agree with them than of those who differ. The result of an approach that relies in varying degrees on anecdotes, on selective and unexamined statistical studies, and on expert opinion chosen to support conclusions already reached is a body of literature that uniformly endorses the five basic propositions about globalization with which we started, even as it disagrees about who wins and who loses from the process, and what can and should be done to influence its future course.

There is a glaring need for a clear, inclusive, digestible presentation of the wide range of systematic data that addresses the question of the likely future of globalization. This absence is particularly unfortunate, since those data shine a bright light on many of the fundamental issues. Unlike anecdotes or selective citation of experts, this kind of evidence can clear up many of the points at issue and put the discussion on a more factual, less emotional plane. This book is our effort to meet that need.

Still, no matter how well illuminated by data, globalization is a complex process with many moving and interacting parts. To keep the analysis on track, we have organized the book around the same central propositions introduced earlier. Before we get to the question of whether globalization is good or bad, it is important to know:

1. Will it increase or diminish in economic importance?
2. Does the crucial issue of achieving economic development and higher living standards depend more on global or local conditions?
3. To what extent are workers in rich countries likely to be affected by globalization?
4. How will business be influenced, and how are various strategies likely to play out in a global world?
5. What are the full implications of financial market globalization?

Finally, we ask whether there are any basic challenges raised by globalization that have been largely ignored but need to be addressed. The chapters in this book take up these questions in sequence. The answers may surprise you.

Chapter 1

It May Be News, But It Isn't New

A Brief History of Globalization

Globalization has a history, though it is hard to say precisely when it began. The Roman Empire doesn't qualify as global, because despite its enormous expanse and a certain level of economic activity between the parts, most of the world was still outside its boundaries and most production remained local. The British Empire in 1815, after Waterloo, had an even larger footprint, but international trade was insignificant and one of the original purposes of the empire was to give Britain privileged access to its colonies, as both sources of raw material and markets for its goods. However, later in the nineteenth century, Britain led the move to reduce barriers to trade. At the same time, the telegraph, steam transportation, and other technologies shrank the time and the cost of moving information and goods, and people began to migrate in large numbers. Economic and social activity across national boundaries grew in importance and began to attract notice.

In his classic book, *The Great Illusion*, British writer Norman Angell argue that, due to what we now call *globalization*, the nation-state had declined as a factor in economic performance. The two great economic forces, capital and labor, had become fully internationalized, cutting across state borders. According to Angell, international finance had "become so independent and interwoven with trade and industry . . . that political and military power can in reality do nothing for trade . . . and all these factors are making rapidly for the disappearance of state rivalries."[1] As a consequence, wars could no longer be fought profitably and were therefore becoming outmoded. Nearly a century later, Thomas Friedman reaffirm this analysis: "As countries [get] woven into the fabric of global trade and rising living . . . standard, the cost of war for the victor and vanquished [becomes] prohibitively high."[2]

Angell received a Nobel Prize in 1933, but he won it for peace, not for prophecy. *The Great Illusion* originally appeared in 1909 and was soon overtaken by events.[3] He was tragically wrong about modern industrial states not going to war against one another, as World War I demonstrated with the blood of millions. But he was also mistaken about a future of ever-increasing economic internationalization and the diminishing importance of national boundaries. The rapid advance of transportation and communication technologies did not lead to a more interdependent economic world, at least not right away. Globalization, whether measured by trade, movements of capital, or emigration, peaked between 1910 and 1920, and then declined steadily for the next 30 to 40 years. Thomas Friedman may prove a better forecaster than Norman Angell, but we think that is unlikely.

Tradable Goods

Trade occurs when people in one country want something provided elsewhere, because it is better, cheaper, or locally unavailable. The growth of trade within any particular category of goods depends on falling transportation, communications, and financing costs. It also depends on the absence of prohibitive government interference, through measures such as tariffs or quotas imposed on imported goods.

Some kinds of output are inherently easier to trade across national boundaries than others; grain travels better than child care, for example. The overall importance of global trade depends on the mix of final demand between easily traded goods and goods that don't travel well. Shifts in demand toward nontraded goods (and services) may outweigh the effects of improvements in transportation, communications, and financing, and government reductions in legislated barriers to trade. In that case, globalization declines as a factor in overall economic life, despite trade-enhancing improvements. A decline of this sort occurred in the 1920s, as trade as a portion of economic output shrank. We think a similar decline is almost certain to happen in the foreseeable future.

The volume and importance of international trade has moved up and down over the last 200 years. Starting early in the nineteenth century, continual improvements in transportation and communications led to a steady growth in the importance of international trade relative to overall economic

Table 1.1   Global Trade as Share of Global Output

Year	Trade as Share of Output	Annual Change
1820	2%	
1875	9%	3%
1910	16%	2%
1920	18%	0%
1950	13%	−1%
1975	22%	2%
2000	30%	1%

SOURCE: A. Estevadeordal, B. Frantz, A.M. Taylor, "The Rise and Fall of World Trade, 1970–1979," *Quarterly Journal of Economics,* May 2003, and International Monetary Fund, *International Financial Statistics.*

activity. From 2 percent of total output in 1820, trade grew to 9 percent by 1875 (a 4.5-fold increase) and then to 18 percent in 1920 (a twofold increase).[4] Table 1.1 presents an abridged view of this history.

Even during this boom period, the law of diminishing returns set in. In the first 55 years, from 1820 to 1875, blockbuster innovations, especially the rapid expansions of the railroads, the emergence of coal-fired steamships to replace sailing vessels, and the invention of the telegraph, generated an annual growth rate for international trade that exceeded the growth of overall output by 3 percent. During the next 35 years, from 1875 to 1910, the growth rate of trade surpassed that of output by 1.7 percent per year. New technologies continued to appear—oil-powered ships, motor transport on land, telephone and radio communications—and existing ones improved. But their effects were less dramatic than the advances at the start of the period. Finally, in the 10 years following Angell's book, from 1910 to 1920, trade grew only 0.3 percent per year more rapidly than output, as the impact of these innovations declined still further.

After 1920, globalization went into reverse for three decades. Certainly, the Depression, in the protectionist policies it spawned, and the great disruption of World War II played a role. But more important were underlying economic developments that changed the mix of outputs in a way that greatly reduced the overall significance of international trade.

Until 1920, the world economy was largely devoted to the production of commodities: raw food and other agricultural products, metals and other minerals, coal, bulk textiles. As late as 1920, expenditures on food accounted for more than 60 percent of total household spending in the United States. But a major shift was in process, a shift that accelerated after 1920. Differentiated manufactures—automobiles, household appliances, electrical equipment, processed foods—came to dominate household spending and economic output.

Two forces spurred this transformation. First, production in agriculture, mining, and metals became much more efficient. Rapid productivity growth drove down both prices and employment in these commodity industries. Even though physical output continued to expand, the value and economic significance of commodity products began a long decline. Second, incomes rose, thanks to improved productivity. Consumers could spend less for the same quantity of basic goods they had previously bought, leaving enough to buy the novel manufactured items that brought variety, convenience, comfort, and status into their lives.

This changing composition of demand affected international trade. The infrastructure of trade—transportation equipment, shipping lines, communications links, agency relationships, marketing programs—had evolved to handle the movement and distribution of commodities, which was uncomplicated. National differences in tastes and requirements for wheat, soybeans, steel, copper, coal, cotton, wool, and the rest were either limited or nonexistent. Shipping could be done in bulk. Prices were well-known and well-defined. Customized local marketing efforts and service support after the sale were rarely required. This system, designed for bulk commodities, proved inadequate to conduct trade in the differentiated manufactures that were capturing increasing amounts of consumer spending.

By their very nature, differentiated products respond to local tastes and specifications, like clothing styles and voltage requirements for electrical equipment. Prices are not set in global commodity markets; they depend on the success of local marketing efforts. So does sales volume. Shipping can require precise packaging and handling. And after-sale support for items like automobiles, appliances, and industrial equipment entails extensive local service and supply networks. It took time to set up this more elaborate commercial infrastructure, and until it was in place, trade suffered.

Both the changes in the composition of economic activity and the consequences for trade are apparent in data for the U.S. economy (Table 1.2). In the two decades from 1900 to 1920, agriculture and mining accounted for roughly 20 percent of U.S. economic output and between 30 and 40 percent of employment, although the employment figures were already declining because of rising productivity. Trade as a fraction of U.S. output increased from 17 percent in 1900 to 24 percent in 1920, a rate slightly faster than the global figures, which were depressed by World War I and its aftermath. Between 1920 and 1930, agriculture and mining fell from 18.5 percent of total U.S. output to 12.6 percent. The relative importance of trade also plummeted; from 24 percent of output in 1920, it dropped to just 11 percent in 1930. Over the next 30 years, trade remained at around 10 percent. Agriculture and mining continued their relative decline, falling to around 8 percent of output in 1960.

Table 1.2   Trade, Agriculture, and Mining in the U.S. Economy

Year	Trade as Share of Output	Agriculture and Mining as Share of Output
1900	17%	21%
1920	24%	19%
1930	11%	13%
1940	9%	12%
1960	10%	8%

SOURCE: *Historical Statistics of the United States.*

Starting in 1950, trade began a steady recovery from the depths to which it had sunk. Given what Adam Smith described as a propensity in human nature "to truck, barter, and exchange one thing for another," it was only a matter of time before businesses learned to sell differentiated products in distant markets. The growth of multinational corporations in the period after World War II allowed branded products, like General Motors cars, Nike shoes, and IBM computers, either to be assembled from parts made in lower-cost manufacturing operations in foreign countries, or to be produced there entirely. Firms like Siemens, Daimler-Benz, Cadbury Schweppes, Néstles, and Sony acquired the skills to market their product globally. At the same time, a political climate generally favorable to international commerce permitted the steady reduction in tariffs and other barriers to international trade. (To put the importance of trade policy in perspective, we should bear in mind that a favorable government climate in the 1920s could not compensate for the effects of changes in the mix of economic activity, and that trade began to revive in the 1950s, well before the big reductions in barriers in the 1960s.) As a consequence, between 1950 and 1975, trade once again grew more rapidly than overall output, by a margin of over 2 percent per year (Table 1.1).

And once again this growth was subject to diminishing returns. In the next 25 years, the advance of trade over output reverted to 1.2 percent per year.

From Goods to Services

Since 1950, there has been a steady shift in global economic activity from differentiated manufactures to services, a transformation that mirrors the move early in the twentieth century from commodities to differentiated manufactures (Table 1.3). Manufacturing, which at the start of the period accounted for around 32 percent of economic output in the United States, had by 2000 declined by half, to just under 16 percent. If this trend continues, manufacturing will represent 4 percent of output in the United States by the end of this century, which is less than agriculture and raw material today. The share of the service sector, broadly defined to include transportation,

Table 1.3   Share of GDP by Industry in the United States

Year	1950	1970	1990	2000	Trend
Manufacturing	32%	27%	18%	16%	Declining
Agriculture, mining, construction	14%	10%	8%	7%	Declining
Government	10%	16%	14%	12%	Level
Wholesale & retail trade	17%	15%	16%	16%	Level
Transportation, communications	9%	8%	9%	8%	Level
Finance, insurance, real estate	9%	11%	17%	20%	Growing
Services	9%	13%	19%	22%	Growing

SOURCE: *Historical Statistics of the United States, Statistical Abstract of the United States.*

communications, utilities, and government services, along with health care, education, retail sales, and all the other activities generally included, rose from 54 percent to 78 percent of the total economy during the same 50 years ending in 2000. Because these service goods are inherently more difficult to provide across national boundaries, continuing expansion of this sector will reduce the impact of globalization, much as the earlier growth of the complex manufactures did in the period after 1920.

Growth in productivity, this time in manufacturing, is again primarily responsible for this reordering of economic activities. This productivity growth has been rapid. Thanks to computer-based advances in automation, there is reason to think the pace will continue. Between 1980 and 2000, manufacturing productivity in the United States grew at an average of 3.4 percent per year, much faster than the overall annual increase of 1.8 percent in all nonfarm businesses. The gap has not closed in the years after 2000. As long as this trend continues, the relative prices of manufactured goods will fall, as will employment in manufacturing, even if demand for manufactured goods keeps pace with overall consumer demand.

In fact, for many years, as incomes have risen, consumers have been increasing the share they spend on services and shrinking the share going to manufactures. In 1970, households in the United States spent 23 percent of their budgets on food, and about 80 percent of that (18 percent of the total) went to buy manufactured food products consumed at home (Table 1.4). By 2000, the total for food had fallen to 15 percent, only two-thirds of which (10 percent of the total) was for eating at home. Clothing expenditures followed the same downward path, as did shelter costs, especially those for home furnishing and household supplies. Moving upward to take up the slack was increased spending on medical care and business, social, and educational services.[5]

Table 1.4 Consumption Expenditures in the United States
(as share of total)

Year	1970	2000
Rent, utilities, service	22%	19%
Furnishings, supplies	7%	3%
Total shelter	*29%*	*22%*
Food at home	18%	10%
Prepared food (eating out)	5%	5%
Total food	*23%*	*15%*
Clothing	10%	6%
Transportation	13%	12%
Medical care	8%	17%
Business, social, & educational service	9%	15%
Recreation	7%	9%
Other	1%	4%
Total	**100%**	**100%**

SOURCE: *Statistical Abstract of the United States.*

Older and richer people spend relatively more of their incomes on housing, education, medical care, and other services. As the population ages and becomes wealthier, these are almost certainly going to continue increasing their share of overall household consumption. Thus, trends in demand in favor of services will reinforce underlying trends in increased productivity and lower costs in manufacturing. The future of manufacturing will look like the past of agriculture and the extractive industries, and it will become an increasingly marginal part of the overall economy, even though there will be no shortage of manufactured goods.

What will this mean for the future of globalization? Manufactures have historically been easier to trade than services, which, in the great majority of cases, are produced and consumed locally, like housing and medical care. If this pattern continues to hold, then we are at an inflection point similar to that of the early 1920s, after which globalization became a diminishing factor in the world economy.

Thomas Friedman, Clyde Prestowitz, Robert Shapiro,[6] and a number of other writers on the subject have argued the opposite. They foresee advances in information technology and communications that will allow—or compel—services to follow the historical path of differentiated manufactures and be provided across national borders as easily as toys, tractors, and topcoats. Don't count on it. A precise examination of the kinds of services that are likely to be in demand in the future suggests that they will be difficult to globalize.

Which Services Remain Rooted?

The largest single area of consumer demand is shelter, including housing and related services and products. By its very nature, housing itself must be supplied locally. Unless Americans, Europeans, or Japanese live in India or China, they will not be offshoring their housing needs. Utilities, household improvements and repairs, and home maintenance services must also be provided locally. Some services, like security monitoring, may be done from abroad, but the installation will be a local service, as will emergency response. Even the monitoring that might be done offshore is likely to be automated through voice response and computer-based decision systems, shrinking the potential global component of this service.

Similar features are at work in medical care. For all the talk of foreign radiologists reading X-rays from the United States,[7] the great majority of health-care activities require direct contact between patient and doctor. For acute care cases and those that can be performed as outpatient procedures, overseas travel is not a real possibility. Nor is it for emergency surgery, where immediate care is necessary. Recurrent treatments for physical therapy, rehabilitation, or long-run custodial care must be done locally, unless patients are to be warehoused overseas, away from family and friends. Day-to-day care and diagnoses associated with office visits are also confined to local providers. Remote diagnosis and prescription of medication may ultimately be practical without direct patient contact. But if these services can be provided remotely, the chances are good that many of them can also be automated either entirely or partially, with voice or visual response systems and computer-based analytical software.

A comparable development has already happened in medical testing. Individual self-test devices that provide instant responses are increasingly available for pregnancy, strep infections, diabetes monitoring, and other conditions. These need only local distribution through pharmacies or other outlets. At the opposite end of the scale, massive centralized facilities perform automated tests on samples that have been collected locally. For these procedures, the greatest part of the human activity involved is devoted to taking and transporting the test samples. In either case, overseas provision of these services is limited.

In searching for globally provided medical services, we are left with only a few genuine cases. One is a mythical army of the night, bargain overseas radiologists who turned out, when someone really looked, to consist of U.S.–board certified doctors who had returned to India,[8] and Nighthawk Radiology, a U.S.-based company using radiologists in Australia, Switzerland, and the United States to provide immediate, first-read services on a limited basis during off-hours for U.S. hospitals.

A second case is the industry called *medical tourism*, which consists of surgery with perhaps a vacation included in places where the medical care is good and the prices are sufficiently below those in the developed countries to more than cover the costs of the trip. The British National Health Service is sending people to India for heart surgery, and Singapore and Thailand are working to become major destinations for treatment, appealing to Americans, Europeans, and Japanese on price and to other Asians on quality. But even if medical tourism grows rapidly, it is highly unlikely that the provision of medical services as a whole will become global in any significant way.[9]

For educational, religious, and social services, outsourcing in the usual sense has never been significant because most of these activities are inherently social. Going to church has always involved going to church with others—the congregation—and the experience cannot be duplicated at a distance, whether by broadcast ministries, the Internet, or any other technological means, at least not with the same emotional resonance. Schools are also social, even custodial, institutions; these features are at least as important as the purely educational ones. It is almost impossible to imagine that children will be provided with effective supervision and socialization over the Internet; it is hard enough to provide them in schools. For older students, the social component is more important than the custodial one, but that still requires direct contact. Imagine American colleges without beer busts, athletic events, and all-night talk sessions. These functions are not going to be outsourced, either domestically or globally. Finally, social services are by definition social, involve direct personal interactions, and are not going to be provided from some distant site.

A future in which distance learning predominates, churches hold services by placing "big brother"-type monitors in parishioners' homes, and people interact largely via Internet sites like MySpace and Facebook, replacing endless teen telephone calls and current network television series, has long been an element, generally a dreaded element, of science fiction. If social networking sites ultimately become a substitute for what people of our generation consider "genuine interactions," that will involve not only progress in technology, but also in evolution. So far, the impact of these developments has been limited.

For example, education has been identified by Thomas Friedman and others as one of the next great areas of global outsourcing. Educators have been entranced by the possibilities of distance learning since before the earliest days of radio and television. The Chautauqua Institute for correspondence education was established in upstate New York in 1883. The first educational radio license was issued to the Latter Day Saints University in 1921. Iowa State University offered the first educational television programs in 1950. The Public Broadcasting System, with its strong educational orientation, was established in 1964. The Open University started in 1971, to provide students in the United Kingdom with courses based on a media mix of television and correspondence units. In 1993, Jones International University became the first accredited online university in the United States. It was followed during the height of the Internet boom in the late 1990s by a plethora of new companies offering online courses, as well as established universities who jumped into the field.

In the face of these technologically advanced methods for delivering instruction, or at least information, education remains overwhelmingly school based and dependent on local teaching. The new technologies have augmented the traditional, school-based processes, but they have not supplanted them. Apart from the custodial and social aspects of education, face-to-face human interaction appears to be an essential part of any effective pedagogical process. The Open University discovered that to accomplish its instructional mission it needed local tutorial centers, where direct interactions between students and instructors could take place.

A 2000–2001 survey of American colleges and universities found that distance learning accounted for just under 2 percent of overall enrollments (3.1 million of around 160 million total, assuming 10 courses per year for a full-time student).[10] Another survey in 2002–2003, this one of elementary and high school students, found that 327 thousand were enrolled in distance education; that figure accounts for less than 1 percent of the more than 50 million students in primary and secondary schools. Looking forward, the U.S. Distance Learning Association, an interested party, projects distance learning to grow by 12 percent per year, and to account for $1.8 billion in spending in 2008. In the 2001–2002 academic year, overall spending by U.S. educational institutions came to $780 billion, so the distance learning component is and will continue to be small. Even the projected growth rate of 12 percent annually is in line with anticipated growth rate in business education and training, of around 10 to 15 percent through 2008.

Despite the isolated tales of tutors in India coaching American students through math classes, meaningful globalization of education, religion, and social services will require major changes in human behavior that are likely to occur slowly, if at all. In the near term, the chief presence of globalization in these areas will continue to be students going abroad to study and religious and social groups, like the Boy Scouts, traveling to international meetings and congresses. The United States and other developed countries are not at a disadvantage in supplying these services. In the 2004–2005 academic year, 206,000 American students studied abroad—overwhelmingly in other developed countries—compared to 565,000 who came into the United States to study. China and India, whatever their advantages in other areas, are unlikely to become the destinations of choice for U.S. students going abroad any time soon.

Recreation and restaurant meals together account for 14 percent of household expenditures, compared to 10 percent for purchased food prepared at home. These activities are not moving overseas. People go to local movies, local clubs, and local sporting events, and when they eat out or order in, they do that locally as well (excepting of course the meals eaten during overseas travel). Nobody calls Naples to get a pizza delivered. Entertainment brought into the home via the airways or landlines is generally provided locally, except for all the American movies, television shows, and recorded music that are both consumed and deplored in other countries. Another major exception is manufactured imports, such as televisions and other electronic gear, sports equipment, food products, beverages, and other goods that have been imported for many years and are now declining in economic importance.

Much has been made of some parts of these services that can be supplied remotely and even globally: ticket purchasing, order taking, support services of various kinds. The voice at the McDonald's drive-through window may originate in Denver or Mumbai and transmit the order back to the local store. But these activities comprise a small and probably shrinking share of the money spent on recreation and restaurant services. For activities to be provided remotely, they must generally be routine—that is, organized into a standard and often mechanical procedure. If they can be defined by a routine, they can be automated. If they can be automated, their costs and economic significance are likely to decline, whether they are handled by a computer or a lower-paid worker in a remote location.

As with cable and broadcast television, the infrastructure parts of utilities, telecommunications, and transportation—transmission lines, roads, installed rail tracks—must be provided locally. The capital equipment for these functions has been subject to global competition for many years, and like other manufactured items, it is declining in cost and importance. With some of this equipment, such as automobiles or construction gear, the manufactured inputs are heavy, costly to transport, and can be made with less and less labor. These features allow competitive production in high-wage economies, like the Japanese automobile transplant factories that are profitable manufacturers within the United States.

Government services such as police, fire, road maintenance, parks, welfare, licensing, other administrative functions, and homeland security will continue to be provided locally, with rare exceptions. Some service functions may be purchased abroad. But again, what can be handled remotely can be automated and at diminishing cost. Also, a preference for "buying local" is not going to vanish from governments subject to political control. To expect substantial offshoring of government services is not realistic.

Finally, there is the broad area of business and financial services—banking, credit cards, brokerage (including real estate and insurance as well as stocks and bonds), legal, accounting, and other more specialized functions. These are purchased both by households and other businesses. Because these sectors, especially the whole area of finance, have received so much attention in the globalization debate, we will deal with them extensively in Chapter 5. We are going to describe them briefly here to complete this survey of the likely future of the globalization of services.

These services generally fall into three categories. The first is high-level, high-value, generally professional services, usually of some complexity and with content specific to the consumer. Lawyers, financial advisors, both personal and institutional bankers, accountants, and many business consultants fall into this category. These services involve a large element of direct communication and mutual trust between the professional and the customer. The services tend to be customized. No one who has a choice is going to rely on a divorce lawyer or tax accountant or financial planner who was located in the Yellow Pages or on the Internet and works from Bangalore or Guangdong. (To a lesser extent, the same preferences apply domestically; people in Minneapolis don't use divorce lawyers in Phoenix.) These kinds of services are not about to be globalized in the foreseeable future.

The second set of services are more routine but still need major local facilities either for collecting or distributing information. Banking and mortgage lending typically fall into this category. Banks must have some local presence to provide services, and mortgage lenders need to be well-informed about local real estate conditions. (The recent debacle in the securitized mortgage market, through which banks and other companies could initiate mortgages and then package them into opaque debt instruments to offload onto remote, uninformed bond buyers, underscores the risks of investing without local knowledge. It also highlights the ability of motivated financial professionals to sell practically anything.) Both must market their services locally, even if some elements of client servicing are done remotely. These services are largely locally provided, though perhaps through divisions that are subsidiaries of a multinational parent, like HSBC.

Third, there are the most routine services—back-office information processing, transcription, order entry, and basic administrative functions—which can be centralized and provided remotely. Like all routine functions, these are increasingly being automated; think of ATMs, interactive web sites, and personal computer programs for financial management and tax preparation. With automation comes lower costs and less economic importance, especially as a source of employment. The

jobs being eliminated in these functional areas are disappearing
for reasons that have little to do with, and long preceded, current anxieties about global outsourcing. We provide fuller detail
on employment patterns in Chapter 3.

Putting all these trends together, it is unlikely that globalization in the form of international outsourcing within the
various segments of the service sector will offset the trend in
demand and output away from globalized manufacturing
and toward locally produced services. The segments within
the broader service sector that might move offshore are both
limited and declining in importance, since they are the same
functions that can be automated. We are currently in a period
like that from 1920 to 1950, in which changes in the composition of economic activity—then the trend toward differentiated manufacturing; now the move toward locally produced
and consumed services—outweigh the impact of improving
transportation and communications on globalization. It is likely
to be a period in which economic globalization declines in
importance. The developed countries that will be hardest hit
by globalization are those such as France, Germany, Italy, and
Japan, which try to sustain significant employment in manufacturing. Those countries that embrace a service-centered economy—the United States, the United Kingdom, Denmark, and
some others—should have a better experience. For these countries, the negative impact of globalization on employment and
on economic activity in general will prove to have been more
of a twentieth rather than a twenty-first century episode.

Why So Newsworthy?

We have followed the course of globalization from its initial
emergence in the late nineteenth century to the decline starting after World War I and its reemergence in the decades

following World War II. We have described the goods and services that have been traded across national boundaries over these periods, and we have also identified the trends in national economies that describe the waning significance of physical goods and the growing importance of services, at least in more developed countries. If these trends persist, and if, as we believe, most services continue to be locally produced and delivered, then globalization in the years ahead will be a less disruptive force in overall economic life than it has been over the last two or three decades. We are not forecasting a decline in international trade, certainly not as measured by volume. We are predicting that the value of that trade as a part of total economic activity will certainly not increase at the rate it has in the past, and should eventually decline.

If we are correct, and globalization is indeed yesterday's news, what accounts for the overwrought treatment that outsourcing, offshoring, and other aspects of globalization receive in the major media? One possible explanation is the impact of recent technological developments on the various media, including the people who work for these organizations and the people who own them. The emergence of the Internet as a decentralized, low-cost source of information has cut heavily into the demand for traditional products like newspapers, magazines, and television. The Internet supplies information more quickly, in a more targeted fashion, and, by allowing comparisons with and among these traditional sources, shows how redundant many of them are. At the local level, news used to be the exclusive property of the local newspaper, which may also have owned the television and radio stations. By lowering the costs at which independent, local providers of information can operate, the Internet has increased competition for local news coverage and has loosened the monopoly hold the traditional media had on businesses that wanted to advertise locally.

These changes have undermined the economic position of traditional media. The people whose lives are most affected, those who gather, edit, and report the news and the owners of the companies for which they work, have reflexively placed the blame on foreigners and other outsiders, just as many others who experienced the wrenching changes wrought by economic transformations have traditionally done—hence the emphasis on the negative and powerful impact of globalization. In fact, these changes in technology have tended to support local rather than global production of information. For example, Internet music downloads have increased the proportion of locally produced songs on local hit parades.[11] As a result, some leading international media companies, like News Corp and Reuters, have begun to adjust and to think of themselves as *multilocal* organizations living increasingly on specialized and local information, rather than global companies providing general information around the world.

Chapter 2

Countries Control Their Fates

How Little Globalization Explains

When Margaret Lee's[1] parents married in 1968, a single small cake was the only luxury gracing their austere wedding celebration. There were no bridal clothes for the event, no honeymoon trip to a picturesque location, or to any location at all. After the ceremony, they returned to a small, crowded apartment with little privacy, limited heat, and no amenities like hot running water. Their diet consisted almost entirely of rice and other grains. Despite the equivalent of a college education for each of them, they held menial jobs for which they received wages barely above subsistence. Their meager existence was typical of the overwhelming majority of mainland Chinese.

By 2000, they had moved into their own apartment; although small by western standards, it was lavish compared to their circumstances 30 years earlier. They had reliable electricity, central heating, and modern appliances. Their varied diet included meat and seafood, and they owned extensive wardrobes. The medical care they received was leagues beyond what had been available to them in 1968. They now had the opportunity and the means to travel, and their daughter was able to pursue an advanced journalism degree in the United States.

At first glance, this developmental miracle, taking place over a mere three decades and within a single generation, seems to capture the upside of globalization. Examined more closely, the fairytale story of China rising demonstrates less the power of globalization than its limitations. The principal force that enriched the lives of Margaret's parents emerged within China itself. The government relaxed its rigid Maoist control of economic activity, allowing private enterprises to bloom and operate within a market system. People who responded to the incentives and seized the opportunities now were able to retain the rewards of their efforts and to profit from the increased economic activity that followed. The ultimate result was a transformation of low-performing, low-productivity, state-run enterprises into companies equal to those in the developed world.

Without doubt, access to foreign markets facilitated changes in the quality and scope of Chinese manufacturers. But rapid growth in trade has been a consistent feature of the global economy since the 1950s. First Europe, then Japan, then South Korea and the other Asian Tigers were able to sell their products in international markets, well before globalization became an obsessive focus of public discourse. China remained outside this commercial world until local decisions—the abandonment of Maoist economics if not single-party politics—removed these self-imposed barriers.

A similar story applies to India. Before 1980, it had utterly failed to take advantage of the opportunities offered by growing global trade. Though hardly Maoist, India lived under a regime locals referred to as the "Permit Raj," which stifled enterprise and development through extensive regulation, relegating the economy to "the Hindu rate of growth." Individual economic success was frowned upon. Only with substantial deregulation and the growth of a more positive public view toward enterprise did India begin to experience the kind of economic miracle that occurred in China. As in China, the essential changes were local, not global.

More evidence of the primacy of local forces in spurring economic growth comes from comparing India and China with countries that had been their peers—impoverished and underdeveloped—only two or three decades ago. Argentina, Mexico, Ghana, and a host of other countries did not follow the paths of India and China, even though the same international economic conditions, the same global markets, were equally available to them. If globalization were a universal and irresistible force, sweeping everything before it, then we would not witness the enormous disparities in economic growth that have separated China, India, and a few other, largely Asian, countries from the stragglers. If, in the midst of globalization, some countries flourish while others flounder, the reasonable conclusion is that local features— things other than globalization—must be responsible for the diverse results.

Who Calls the Shots?

To gauge the importance of globalization itself, we need to look at its average impact on the world as a whole, or at least its average impact on categories of countries, like highly developed or less-developed ones. If common effects are large and growing as globalization increases, then globalization is indeed the omnipotent force that many have claimed. But if local differences in standards of living, both the levels and the rates of change, are large relative to these global trends, then, despite all the hyperventilation over globalization, local conditions and local choices are more important than global ones. If some poor countries, like Vietnam and Botswana, have a much better time of it than the average of other poor countries with similar endowments, the implication is that local conditions dominate common, global influences.

The evidence is strongly on the side of local circumstances. Throughout the course of economic history, countries have repeatedly experienced markedly different degrees of prosperity in the face of the trends in globalization described in the previous chapter. Local disturbances at the edges of the pond, such as the sudden emergence of China and India as economic players of consequence, have been far more powerful than any global forces affecting the pond as a whole. Ironically, the present concern over what globalization may do to jobs, profits, and even national economies has been sparked by changes in these two countries that are local in origin. Evidence both past and present suggests that countries will respond differently to the challenges flowing from China and India. Some will emulate, some will fulminate, and some will accommodate to suit their own needs. There will be little that is universal—global—as countries adjust to the rise of these and other new economic powers.

Historically, globalization has never been powerful enough to produce anything like a uniform response across all the countries affected by it. In the late nineteenth and early twentieth centuries, the economies of the United States, Northern Europe, Great Britain, and the dominion countries of the

British Empire—Canada, Australia, New Zealand—grew much faster than the rest of the world. Argentina was also a striking success. By 1913, after decades of rapid globalization, the developed world consisted almost entirely of this handful of countries. In Asia, only Japan had seen much economic growth. Latin America, with the exceptions of Argentina, Uruguay, Chile, and the southern parts of Brazil, was also poor. Explanations offered to account for these differences emphasize cultural, political, historical, and geographic circumstances. We do not need to select among them to point out that they all are local in nature, and that they have more than withstood whatever homogenizing impact globalization may have had.

After World War II, the devastated countries of western Europe grew faster than Great Britain, where destruction had been much less extreme, and even faster than the United States, which not only had escaped unscathed but also had added all the new plants built for war production to its capital stock. Argentina, Uruguay, and southern Brazil lagged behind. Japan, by contrast, recovered so strongly that by the 1980s, many were predicting it would come to lead the world economy. In the last third of the twentieth century, other Asian countries—South Korea, Singapore, Taiwan, Hong Kong—joined the club of developed nations. Malaysia and Thailand were knocking on the door. In southern Europe, Spain, Portugal, Italy, and to a lesser extent Greece, became rich. In the 1990s, Ireland, which had stagnated for centuries, emerged in the blink of an eye as one of the most successful economies anywhere—a Celtic Tiger.

Economic growth in Mexico and most of Latin America, which had done well in the two decades after World War II, flattened out and even turned negative after 1965. On the other hand, both China, starting around 1980, and India, a decade later, began their rapid ascent. At the same time, Japan lost its dynamism and suffered an extended period of stagnation in the 1990s and into the current century. All these countries were operating in the same world, so global conditions cannot account for the diversity of their experiences.

The ups and downs of globalization have had little impact on economic growth. For the world as a whole, the rate of increase in average standards of living was approximately the same in the years of declining globalization between 1913 and 1950 as it was during the years of rapid globalization— indicated by increasing trade as a fraction of overall output— between 1820 and 1913[2] (Table 2.1). Europe and Asia, which were severely damaged by two world wars, experienced declining rates of economic growth in the latter period, even as it accelerated in the United States and Latin America during the same years. The revival of global trade and investment after 1950 did coincide with a marked improvement in standards of living across the world. But after 1973, despite continued global integration, rates of growth declined for the world as a whole. Quite apart from the difficult question of whether growth drives global trade or global trade drives growth, there has been no consistently strong relationship, positive or negative, between global economic integration and aggregate global economic growth.

Table 2.1   Annual Growth in GDP per Capita

Period	World	United States	Europe	Asia (non-Japan)	Latin America
1820–1913	0.89%	1.56%	1.12%	0.11%	0.89%
1913–1950	0.91%	1.61%	0.76%	0.02%	1.43%
1950–1973	2.93%	2.45%	4.08%	2.92%	2.52%
1973–1998	1.33%	1.99%	1.78%	3.54%	0.99%

SOURCE: Angus Maddison, *The World Economy: A Millennial Perspective* (Paris: Development Centre of the Organization for Economic Co-operation and Development), © 2001.

An Inadvertent Experiment

After World War II, many regions that had previously been relatively homogeneous ended up on different sides of the socialist/capitalist divide. Germany is the most clear-cut example, but other places were also separated into matched pairs of one socialist and one capitalist economy. Thirty years later, the consequences of this experiment were obvious. The countries that ended up with capitalist economic systems fared much better than their socialist counterparts, even though some of them had actually been poorer at the start of this period. Finland may have been the poorest of the Baltic countries, worse off than Lithuania, Latvia, or Estonia. Austria was less heavily industrialized than Czechoslovakia. Spain, a Catholic country with a largely agricultural economy, was poorer than Poland, also Catholic and agricultural. Taiwan was one of the more backward provinces of China and for years had been a colony of Japan. Thailand was probably no richer than Vietnam, Cambodia, or Laos. North Korea included the more heavily industrialized parts of the Korean peninsula.

By the early 1990s, the socialist regimes in most of these countries had unraveled. When reasonably accurate economic statistics finally became available, they revealed stark differences between economies that had been similar at the start of the period (Table 2.2). The standard of living, measured by per capita GDP, was generally more than twice as high—sometimes considerably more than twice—in the countries with capitalistic economies. Life expectancies were on average five years longer. To make that statistic more graphic, it is as if, in a country with an average life expectancy of 75 years, one-eighth of the population suddenly began to die at age 35.

There are two conclusions to draw from these comparisons. First, socialist economic institutions were marked failures

Table 2.2 Quality of Life Comparisons, 1992–1994 ($US)

	Formerly Centralized			Noncentralized		
Region	Country	Per Capita GDP	Life Expectancy	Country	Per Capita GDP	Life Expectancy
Baltic	Lithuania, Latvia, Estonia	7,800	70.4	Finland	16,150	76.2
Middle Europe	Czech Republic	7,350	73.5	Austria	17,500	76.9
Agricultural Europe	Poland	4,920	73.1	Spain	13,125	77.9
China	China	2,500	68.1	Taiwan	12,070	75.5
Southeast Asia	Vietnam, Laos, Cambodia	870	55.3	Thailand	5,970	68.4
Korea	North Korea	920	70.1	South Korea	11,270	70.9
Average		4,060	68		12,681	74.3

SOURCE: *The World Factbook.*

in a variety of settings. Second, and more important for our argument, these differences are the consequences of local conditions, and they dwarf any differences attributable to global trends. This natural experiment highlights the variability of economic growth rates among countries and, therefore, the relative weakness of worldwide forces.

Because the figures in the table come from the early postsocialist period, they might reflect the difficulties of "shock" transitions from well-performing socialist economies to capitalist ones. But that explanation is clearly far-fetched. The countries with relatively painless transitions, like China and the Baltic states, were still poorer than their nonsocialist counterparts, as were those that had a sudden and bumpy ride, like Czechoslovakia (then including the Czech Republic and Slovakia). Vietnam and North Korea, which had not yet made the transition, lagged even further behind their capitalist neighbors. In addition, the accuracy of the pretransition statistics, which show living standards that deteriorate with the end of socialism, is suspect. Take the case of North Korea. The output-per-capita figures in Table 2.2 are western estimates. They show a marked advantage to South Korea. The life-expectancy numbers were provided by the North Korean government. They show approximate parity, despite North Korea's experience of one of the worst famines in human history.

The Uneven Course of Manufacturing

The impact of local conditions also influences particular economic sectors within and across national economies. Consider the experience of manufacturing performance in the United States, both in absolute terms and relative to that of other large, industrial economies. Between 1946 and 1970, U.S. productivity in manufacturing grew at an annual rate of 3.0 percent. Then, for the next 10 years, growth slowed to 1.4 percent per year. Starting in 1980, it revived to reach an annual rate of 3.3 percent. This recovery has been attributed to improvements in computing and information technologies, which allowed the automation of many manufacturing processes.

But that explanation is undercut by the fact that other advanced industrial countries, with equal access to the same technologies, did not benefit from the same boost to productivity. Looking at Table 2.3, from 1970 to 1980, the growth of productivity in the United States lagged behind Japan, Germany, and Italy, and was virtually even with Canada and the United Kingdom. By the end of the 1980s, the United States had improved its relative position substantially. It now was ahead of Germany and Canada, level with Italy, and had narrowed the gap with Japan. Only Britain, undergoing a radical economic transformation under Margaret Thatcher, had improved relative to the United States. On average, the swing in relative productivity growth was 1.9 percent per year, almost exactly equal to the 2 percent absolute productivity improvement over time in the United States. Whatever was responsible for both the absolute and relative growth in productivity, it was not global.

Table 2.3 Annual Productivity Growth in Manufacturing Relative to the United States (National Productivity Growth minus U.S. Productivity Growth)

Period	1970–1980	1985–1991
Japan	5.2%	2.3%
Germany	2.0%	−1.1%
Canada	0.2%	−2.6%
Italy	2.4%	0.0%
United Kingdom	0.2%	1.1%

SOURCE: Organization for Economic Co-operation and Development (OECD).

Even though the technology was widely available, the ability of countries to put it to use varied from place to place and from time to time. Again, local conditions appear to shape these significant differences over time and among countries.

The Recipe for Productivity Growth

Gross economic growth can occur simply because the population, especially the labor force, gets larger or because it works more hours. But the growth that matters for economic well-being is growth in productivity, getting more output for each hour worked. Were it not for productivity growth in agriculture, the bulk of humankind—a much smaller bulk than we actually constitute—would still be tilling fields. Productivity growth has been the engine pulling the train of humanity out of poverty.

Economists have labored long and hard to identify the sources of past productivity growth, in part to enlighten policy makers and improve current approaches for alleviating poverty. The three factors that have been cited most frequently are capital accumulation in the form of more equipment per worker, improved labor quality, and new technology. It is easy to see why increasing any of these resources should make workers more productive.

Accepting for the moment this perspective, most of these factors are predominantly local in nature. Education takes place overwhelmingly within countries. Except for immigration, which has always been of marginal importance for economies like Japan, China, India, Western Europe, and the Asian tigers, a country's labor force is locally produced. Capital accumulation through investment is also predominantly local in origin, to a degree that will shock those who see international capital as a powerful and uncontrolled force. (Chapter 5 discusses this topic in more detail.) Only technology is, in theory at least, globally available.

But there is a problem with this approach. The three conventional factors, however logical and even obvious, do not begin to account for the historical experience in countries ranging from the United States to China. In the recipe for productivity growth, a key ingredient has been left out.

If investment, education, and technology, as represented by research and development, were indeed the major sources of increased productivity, then the United States has been in trouble for many years. It has had a low savings rate, which implies a low rate of capital accumulation. Its educational system, especially at the primary and secondary levels, is under constant censure for failing to provide the literacy and numeracy skills required of a modern workforce, and for trailing the schools of other prosperous and some not-so-prosperous countries. And its investment in research and development has fallen behind that of other developed countries. Critics have long predicted that the low quality of the labor force in the United States will lead to the migration of jobs, especially to Asia, where better employees with more modern capital equipment work harder for less money. (We will examine this issue in the next chapter.) Critics have also claimed that the United States is rapidly abdicating technological leadership to the rest of the developed world, and that the failure to save and invest will consign American companies to the losing side in competitive global markets.

Fortunately for the United States, recent history contradicts these gloomy forecasts. The profits of U.S. corporations have been at historic highs, measured as a fraction of total output. Productivity growth in the United States (Table 2.4) has surpassed that of its major industrial competitors in Japan, Canada,

Table 2.4 Productivity Growth Total, 1996–2001

Country	Change in Output per Worker	Change in Hours per Worker	Change in Output per Hour
United States	11.4%	−2.2%	13.6%
Canada	9.6%	2.2%*	7.4%
Japan	6.4%	−2.1%	8.5%
Germany	1.0%	−8.5%**	9.5%
United Kingdom	7.2%	−1.0%	8.2%
Italy	6.3%	−0.3%	6.6%
France	5.2%	−4.0%	9.2%

* Hours paid.
** Hours paid, major statistical revision in 2000.
SOURCES: European Community Statistical Annual; U.S. Department of Commerce; U.S. Department of Labor; Canadian Government Statistics.

and Europe. And unemployment rates are near their historic lows. Given this actual performance, at least one other ingredient must have been at work to account for these successes. And that ingredient must have been significant enough to more than compensate for the shortfalls in savings and investment, education, and research and development.

Importance of Incremental Improvements

The mystery ingredient has been the steady accumulation of small operational improvements, taking place in a largely decentralized fashion within individual establishments throughout the economy. It works through the steady diffusion of seasoned technologies and their increasingly effective application, not from the sudden availability and widespread adoption of new technologies. It does not depend on the arrival of cohorts of highly educated new workers, although minimum levels of education are essential, but on the accumulation of on-the-job learning by existing workers. Finally, although some investment is essential, the efficiency with which capital is used is far more important than the gross amount of capital committed. The most important force driving this incremental growth in productivity is the sustained attention of managers and workers, their continual quest for improvements in operations. By its very nature, this ingredient of productivity growth depends on local circumstances; it is found on the shop floor, in the back office, and at the loading dock. What happens globally is largely irrelevant.

The strength of this ingredient becomes apparent when we compare productivity among essentially identical businesses. In theory, similar businesses with equal access to capital, labor markets, and technology should operate at roughly equal levels of productivity. In fact, productivity differs widely among similar firms. The best-run companies in an industry can operate two to three times more efficiently than the average for the group. For example, in 1991, it cost Connecticut Mutual Insurance Company $2.09 to process every $100 of life insurance premiums; Phoenix Mutual spent $1.56. But both of them trailed Northwestern Mutual, whose costs were $0.63, by an enormous margin.

A similar example comes from the performance of the Bell Operating Companies (BOCs) after the breakup of AT&T in the mid-1980s. (Table 2.5). These BOCs were siblings. All of them used the same equipment, produced by Western Electric, the same technology, from Bell Labs, and hired labor under the same national contract with uniform wages and work rules. They operated in similar environments, a mix of urban and suburban territories. Yet for both overall costs and particular operations, the most efficient company (Bell of Pennsylvania) had cost levels up to 50 percent less than the least efficient

Table 2.5 Performance of the Bell Operating Companies

Cost per Access Line ($)

Company	1988	1991	Change
N.Y. Tel	531	564	6.2%
U.S. West	489	401	−18.0%
Bell of Penn	368	388	5.4%

Customer Service Cost per Access Line

Company	1988	1991	Change
N.Y. Tel	42	46	10.6%
U.S. West	39	40	6.0%
Bell of Penn	30	36	22.3%

SOURCE: FCC Form M Report.

(New York Telephone). Other studies have found variations of these magnitudes between manufacturing plants, between service businesses, and even between individual service operations, like the issuance of bank credit cards. These differences are unrelated to any observed differences in investment per worker, labor force quality, or the technology employed.

These discrepancies indicate that most firms operate substantially below their potential productivity level. They strongly suggest that productivity growth is more likely to come from exploiting this unrealized potential—catching up with the best firm's performance—than from any dramatic innovations that might become available. Additional evidence for this claim comes from the experience of firms under stress from shifting labor market conditions. In the late 1980s, the engineering industry in the United Kingdom negotiated with its unions a reduction in the work week of from five to four days. Existing hourly rates were to remain the same. The goal of the contract was to increase total employment for union members, many of whom had been out of work. But the law of unintended consequences intervened. Employment actually declined substantially, as managers, faced with a sudden reduction in available work-hours, responded by realizing efficiencies that more than compensated for the decline in time worked.

Also, rates of productivity improvements are largely uncorrelated with overall productivity levels. The more efficiently managed firms seem to have as much room for improvement as the laggards. U.S. West outpaced the less-efficient New York Telephone in reducing cost per access line. Northwestern Mutual improved its operating efficiency as much as or more than its competitors. Opportunities for improvements in productivity are available to the best-run firms without running into constraints from labor force quality, investment capital, or existing technologies.

Tell Me Again: Why Is China Rising?

A careful look at the history of changes in rates of productivity growth over time, both for firms and countries, supports the idea that it is management's ability to exploit this unachieved potential that drives most improvements. China is currently the obvious example of a country that has experienced a sustained surge in economic growth, underpinned by improvements in productivity. One standard explanation, familiar to anyone acquainted with the debate over comparative economic performance (e.g., the United States versus Europe or Japan or China or India), is the excellence of the Chinese educational system. According to one columnist, "One reason China is likely to overtake the United States as the world's most important country in this century is that China puts more effort into building human capital than we do."[3] The writer describes the enormous improvements in his wife's ancestral village over the past quarter century: more schools, more students, more hours in class, standards far above those of the best elementary and secondary schools in the United States, and a hunger for education among the population. Another town he visited that had no colleges 20 years ago now has four universities, and almost 60 percent of college-aged students are enrolled. If the United States is not to fall behind, it will have to respond as it did to the "launch of Sputnik in 1957 and raise its own educational standards to meet the competition."

The implication is that the Chinese miracle of the past quarter century has been driven by Chinese excellence in formal education. The column explicitly states that the continuation of this trend will soon make China the world's greatest power. This argument is implausible as history and unreliable as a forecast of the future.

The problem with attributing China's surge in productivity growth to a simultaneous improvement in education is that the timing is all wrong. The figures in Table 2.6 present a sketch of China's reported total and per-capita output growth per year, starting in 1975. Clearly, growth accelerated in the 1980s and has remained high since then. However, children entering school in 1980 would have had 10 years of education by 1990. By 1995, only five yearly cohorts of graduates of the new system would have joined the labor force, where, assuming a

Table 2.6 Annual Growth in Output, 1975–2005

Period	Total Output	Output per Capita
1975–1980	5.5%	4.1%
1980–1985	9.7%	8.4%
Mid-1990s	11.0%	10.0%
Since then	10.0%	10.0%

SOURCE: *The World Factbook, Statistical Abstract of the United States.*

working career of 40 years, they mixed with 35 annual cohorts of older workers who had not benefited from the improved education. The ability of the youngest one-eighth of the labor force to boost overall productivity would have been very limited. Educational improvements play out slowly, over time.

The rapid transformation China experienced starting around 1980 cannot plausibly be attributed to educational reforms. Instead, the explanation almost certainly lies in changes in workplace management that affected the entire labor force within a short period of time. These changes were the direct consequence of the reforms in incentives and management structures that emerged when the stifling hand of the state was relaxed with the abandonment of Maoist economic philosophy. This cultural revolution in managerial processes occurred before educational improvement could transform the labor force and without massive increases in capital investments. The history of China over the past three decades argues that managerial factors are far more important in productivity growth than are educational ones.

The future may be different, and if China achieves superior educational performance, that may propel it to greatest-nation status. However, the last time prognoses like this were offered was in the 1980s, when they predicted Japanese ascendancy and American decline. They did not prove very accurate, as Japan suffered more than a decade of economic stagnation while the United States recovered its dynamism. Similar forecasts about China may experience the same fate.

Episodic Improvements and Retreats

At the level of the firm, improvements in productivity tend to be highly episodic. Companies like Dell Computer find they have lost their competitive edge and respond by refocusing themselves on improving efficiency. They reduce costs rapidly without any associated reduction in output, which is the very definition of growth in productivity. If Dell had been operating at peak efficiency, no such improvements should have been possible (nor would they have been necessary). It would have required an infusion of additional capital investments, embodying new technology, or measurable improvements in Dell's labor force to coax more productivity out of the firm's operations. The short time frames that characterize these kinds of efficiency initiatives at Dell and other companies eliminate capital investment and labor force improvements as explanations for the growth spurts.

The key role of management attention accounts for the episodic nature of changes in productivity. It has been observed at the level of the firm, the sector, and the economy as a whole. We have already alluded to the importance of management-directed initiatives to reduce costs within individual companies. Here are additional examples. In the early 1990s, Compaq Computer began to lose its competitive edge to Dell and others (just as Dell has more recently been outperformed by Hewlett-Packard). Compaq's founding managers, engineers by training, had always focused on product innovation rather than efficiency. When they persisted with this policy, they were ousted by the board of directors and replaced by new management that streamlined everything and cut costs to compete more effectively with Dell. They bought components that they had previously produced internally, they redesigned the assembly processes, and they changed the layout of plants to improve the production flow. They cut R&D and speeded up product development. Thanks to these and other changes, within three years Compaq more than tripled its annual sales per employee.[4] None of these improvements depended on advances in technology, on extensive new capital investment, or on an improvement in the quality of the labor force. What mattered was the determination of the board of directors and the new managers to raise efficiency throughout the company's operations.

Productivity can decline just as rapidly when other issues claim management's attention. The credit card division of Citicorp had been widely recognized as an industry leader in operating efficiency. During the recession of 1990–1991, losses from defaults on credit card balances rose rapidly. When the default rates did not return to their prior levels as the economy recovered, management of the division made reducing these credit default losses the top priority. They succeeded in bringing the losses back into line, but at the cost of letting operational efficiency slide throughout the division. Overall costs rose by more than 25 percent in 24 months, without any increase in output (cards issued, billings, etc.), and affected functions such as marketing and payment processes that were remote from credit default reductions. This kind of productivity growth, the negative kind, is inconsistent with the idea that firms operate at optimum efficiency. It does fit the thesis advanced here, that consistent management attention is essential to operational efficiency, which suffers when that attention is diverted elsewhere.[5]

Widely Shared Diversions

Variations in productivity at the national level can also be explained by the degree to which management attention can focus on efficiency. A well-established but not widely discussed aspect of recessions is the permanent loss in productivity growth that occurs. The standard explanation is that firms do not lay off trained workers in numbers comparable to the decline in demand and output because they do not want to risk the permanent loss of workers in whom they have invested so much. This practice is known as *labor hoarding*. One consequence is that measured hours of work do not decline as much as output, so measured productivity declines. If this argument is correct, the trend should reverse itself when the economy recovers. As demand and output rise, new hiring should be unnecessary and measured hours of work should rise less than output, restoring productivity to its previous level. That expected reversal does not occur. A large fraction of the decline is permanent, and there is no above-normal growth in productivity as the economy recovers.

An alternative explanation, one that accounts for this permanent loss, is that managerial attention is diverted during the recession to more pressing issues, like coping with the deteriorating financial position of the firm and the need to reduce output and costs and get rid of excess inventory. The everyday small improvements in operating efficiency that are forgone while management attention focuses on survival are lost forever, not to be recaptured when the economy recovers.

Similar aggregate declines in productivity growth can be observed in the United States starting in the 1970s (Table 2.7), when increasingly intrusive government regulation coupled with inflation placed more demands on the time and attention of corporate managers. Evidence comes from a comparison of relative productivity growth within each presidential administration in the period after World War II. The figures are adjusted for the impact of recessions and compared to the overall postwar average. They correlate negatively with a qualitative impression of the intensity of regulatory intervention associated with each administration, bolstered by a proxy measure, the number of pages in the Federal Register, where the rules and regulations are published.[6] Regulation began to increase under Johnson and accelerated during the Nixon-Ford years, as laws and rules regarding health, worker safety, the environment, and discriminatory hiring practices became more intensive. Productivity growth declined significantly. It reached its nadir during the Carter administration, when regulation, measured by pages in the Register, was most intense. Under Reagan, the Register shrank and productivity growth improved. These trends were marginally reversed under Bush 1. The correlation between regulatory intensity as measured by pages in the Federal Register, and productivity growth, is 90 percent.[7]

The leading role that managerial interventions play in productivity growth limits the impact of globalization as a force. Management is local, not global, and its performance depends on conditions that are themselves overwhelmingly local—the stability of the national economy, the extent to which attention is diverted to dealing with government regulation, the presence of effective competition and incentive structures, adequate infrastructure development, and other local institutional

Table 2.7 Average Annual Productivity Growth and Federal Regulatory Intensity

Administration	Productivity (Relative Growth per Annum)	Average Pages per Annum in the Federal Register (000s)
Truman	1.9%	12
Eisenhower	0.5%	11
Kennedy	1.5%	14
Johnson	1.1%	19
Nixon	0.0%	28
Ford	1.2%	49
Carter	−1.5%	72
Reagan	−0.3%	54
Bush 1	−0.9%	62

SOURCE: Michael van Biema and Bruce Greenwald, "Managing Our Way to Higher Service-Sector Productivity," *Harvard Business Review*, July–August 1997, pp. 87–95.

arrangements. It is no wonder that even in a global world, local factors dominate in determining economic results.

Because locally produced and consumed services constitute a growing share of economic activity, this state of affairs will become increasingly true in the future. There is an obvious element of good news here. The claims of antiglobalization protestors are largely wrong. Local economies are not passive victims of global forces; their futures are effectively in their own hands. Global trends may aid or hinder local progress to a limited extent, but the overwhelming evidence is that global forces cannot prevent well-functioning local economies from developing rapidly.

The other side of this argument is bad news for the pro-globalization camp. Since countries shape their own fates, there are limits to the benefits that even well-intentioned outside agents can bestow, whether in the form of material intervention—trade or aid—or policy advice. Access to global markets can stimulate local demand and local growth, but only if the firms function effectively and score high on productivity and quality. Material assistance may also provide benefits—reduce disease, lower infant mortality, extend life for adults—but it will not generate the kind of developmental progress that transformed the lives of Margaret Lee's parents. That kind of growth depends on productivity improvements that take place within the right—and local—context.

The history of Marshall Plan aid provided by the United States after World War II illuminates the dominance of local factors. The goal of the plan was to accelerate economic recovery in postwar Europe. The idea that the Marshall Plan was central to Europe's growth in this period is so deeply ingrained that we frequently hear calls for a Marshall Plan for Africa or for the Andean countries, or even for less-developed parts of the United States. But a closer look calls into question

the extent to which the Marshall Plan was responsible for
European recovery. It turns out that the levels of aid received
by the major European countries (Table 2.8) had little bearing
on the speed or the size of their recovery.

The United Kingdom received the most aid, despite having
suffered relatively limited damage during the war. Nevertheless,
its economic growth was far slower than the countries on the
continent. West Germany received significant aid only in two
years, 1948 and 1949. It was also subjected to significant trade
restrictions in this period. Yet it recovered more rapidly and
completely than the United Kingdom. So did Italy, which
received relatively little assistance. Japan was required to pay the
cost of the American occupation, which consumed about one-
third of the total government budget in the immediate postwar
years. Yet it, too, had a record of substantial economic growth.

Overall, it is impossible to detect any positive relationship between levels of U.S. postwar aid and rates of national
economic recovery. That makes it hard to contend that even the
Marshall Plan contributed in a major way to local economic
development. And since the Marshall Plan aid was offered in

Table 2.8   U.S. Post–WWII Economic Assistance ($ millions)

Year	U.K.	France	West Germany	Italy	Japan
1946	750	1,158	300	500	367
1947	2,662	588	417	313	469
1948	937	781	1,130	422	372
1949	1,009	765	948	445	521
1950	624	460	467	269	226
1951	118	416	361	268	241
1952	398	343	103	175	36
1953	229	263	35	109	0
Totals	6,727	4,774	3,761	2,501	2,232

SOURCE: *Historical Statistics of the United States.*

the most propitious circumstances—to countries with well-functioning local institutions and highly skilled labor forces—this history does not augur well for the usefulness of other applications of massive external aid.[8]

Regarding the advice that experts from the developed world have offered to poorer countries, there are some common themes that appear to have helped improve productivity. Incentives to reward economic success within market economies, even if those incentives are reduced by taxes, seem to be found in any successful economy. The ability of management to pursué operating efficiency free from overly intrusive governmental or social control also seems important. Competition seems to have been one stimulant for economic growth. A stable economic environment with low inflation also minimizes distracting demands on management attention. But all of these general principles can be shaped by local variations that influence how successful they will be within the specific local environment.

Social arrangements and the force of behavioral norms vary widely across the societies in which economic activity is embedded. In the wake of the East Asian financial crisis of the late 1990s, South Korea, Indonesia, Thailand, and Malaysia were criticized for their systems of "crony" capitalism, which supposedly violated appropriate standards of government non-interference, unfettered competition, and fair play in allocating credit, permits, contracts, and other essentials for running a business. This criticism ignored the long-term record of economic growth that these countries had produced (Table 2.9). Crony capitalism yielded per-capita growth rates above 4 percent a year for at least three decades and generated the kind of improvement in living standards that transformed the lives of millions of people. By any economic measure, it had been an undeniable success. In the aftermath of the crisis, the countries

Table 2.9 Economic Performance under Crony Capitalism

Country	Annual per Capita GDP Growth 1967–1997	Annual Population Growth 1967–1997	Cumulative Economic Growth 1997–2000
South Korea	7.4%	1.4%	13.0%
Thailand	5.0%	1.9%	−2.0%
Indonesia	4.8%	1.9%	−8.0%
Malaysia*	4.4%	2.7%	7.0%

*1970–1997.
SOURCE: International Financial Statistics.

that most successfully resisted a change to their economic systems—South Korea and Malaysia—recovered more rapidly than the countries—Indonesia and Thailand—that embraced reforms sponsored by the International Monetary Fund and other external agencies.

The culture and status of public service also varies greatly across nations. Some countries boast efficient public enterprise, with dedicated, highly motivated, talented employees. Others have weak traditions of public service, and their government-run services are less effective. The record of public telephone companies before and after privatization demonstrates these differences. Performance in Table 2.10 is measured by growth in the number of telephone access lines serviced per company employee. In Indonesia, Brazil, New Zealand, Malaysia, and South Korea, this crude measure of productivity was growing prior to privatization at rates of 10 percent per year or more, signs of well-functioning public enterprises. Privatization brought no average increase in the rate of productivity growth in these countries as a group. In contrast, Australia, Chile, Mexico, and Venezuela had much lower rates of productivity growth prior to privatization. After the systems were privatized, they saw dramatic gains in performance. Clearly the culture and behavioral norms of these two groups of countries were very different, at least regarding public service. Any standardized prescription in favor of privatization ignores these critical differences among countries. Assuming that individual countries are familiar with the capacities of their public enterprises and at least better informed than outsiders, these kinds of decisions are best made locally.

Local differences also come into play in the areas of regulatory policy, finance, and mechanisms for the public provision of services like health care. The negative effects of regulatory intervention on productivity that we discussed earlier may be particularly severe in the United States, where the process has been contentious, unstable, and highly political. Practices in

Table 2.10   Telecommunications Privatization: The Impact on Access Line per Employee

Country	Change 3 Years Preceding Privatization	Change 3 Years Following Privatization	Net Gain
New Zealand	44%	44%	0%
Indonesia	31%	27%	−4%
Brazil	31%	44%	13%
Malaysia	22%	26%	4%
Korea	10%	−6%	−16%
Average	*28%*	*27%*	*−1%*
Australia	−26%	35%	51%
Venezuela	−7%	38%	45%
Chile	1%	34%	35%
Mexico	6%	25%	31%
Average	*−7%*	*33%*	*40%*

SOURCE: International Telecommunications Union.

Europe, which have been more consistent and have involved a high level of cooperation between governments and business, are likely to have had lower costs and consequences. Models of regulation, like pollution pricing, may be more effective in some national situations than others. In raising capital, the United States and the United Kingdom have relied heavily on public financial markets—stocks and bonds—to move resources from passive savings to active investments. By contrast, many European and Asian countries have depended on thick networks of individual relationships, embodied in banks, insurance companies, and other financial institutions, to do the same task. Financial reforms in favor of competition and public markets may well undermine these institutional structures to the detriment of overall economic performance. (This issue is covered in Chapter 5.)

Extensive social welfare systems work well in Europe, Asia, and Canada because social norms restrain people from excessive consumption of these resources. Identical systems may work far less well in countries like the United States, where those social constraints are much weaker (as a nation of immigrants and their progeny, Americans may have been self-selected to put individual advancement above social solidarity). Given these variations, it makes sense that policies be tailored to meet local conditions. Even a casual examination of international cultural differences indicates how unlikely it is that dreams—or nightmares—of a homogeneous global cultural and social environment will come to fruition.

The clear implication of this extensive diversity among nations is that individual countries and their governments must establish their own policies, even in a supposedly global world. They best understand the possibilities and constraints imposed by local conditions, and they have to live with the consequences. The principle of vesting decisions in those most familiar with the relevant conditions is reinforced by the complementary principle that better decisions are made by those who are subject to the costs and benefits of their choices.

What About Free Trade?

Respect for local autonomy applies even in the area of trade policy. Both theory and experience argue against the uniform application of free trade principles. In theoretical models that assume a predetermined technological constraint, rational value-maximizing agents (households and firms), and perfect information, free trade does generally have unambiguous benefits. But under more realistic assumptions, the model acknowledges that free trade may benefit some countries only at the expense of others.

Suppose, as an example, that technology and productivity are not predetermined but evolve over time in response to local activities. If one region has an initial concentration of a particular industry—biotechnology, for instance—then a number of factors will reinforce its advantages in that industry over time. Knowledge of the relevant technologies will tend to pass from one company to another as managers and professionals move among firms or merely interact in local social and professional settings. As knowledge is more effectively shared, it advances more rapidly within that region than in other places. New firms seeking to capitalize on this technological edge and hire managers already equipped with the relevant skills will be drawn to that region, further concentrating the industry. Individuals with expertise in biotechnology also flock to the neighborhood. As the area flourishes, an enlightened government will be able to invest its expanded revenue in improvements in the physical infrastructure and in education, investments that cannot be matched by other, less-favored regions. This possibility exists in theory, and it has been observed in industry clusters such as the computing technology center of Silicon Valley on the San Francisco peninsula.

The other side of this virtuous cycle for the dominant region is stagnation in less-favored places. Imagine a country whose economy consists overwhelmingly of small, widely dispersed farms and craft businesses. Faced with persistent competition from a variety of industries already benefiting from the advantages of operating in established regions, the country may never build up the critical mass necessary to generate technological progress in any sector. Its infrastructure remains underdeveloped, talented individuals leave for opportunities elsewhere, and the government cannot raise enough tax revenue to support even a rudimentary level of education. It seems condemned to a perpetual state of backwardness and poverty. In these circumstances, tariffs that limit overseas competition may, in theory, serve to break this low-growth cycle and help put the country on a path to development.

Experience also argues against the automatic implementation of free trade policies. The United States in the nineteenth and early twentieth centuries, Continental Europe after World War II, Japan, the Asian Tigers, and today's China and India have all prospered behind relatively high, relatively uniform (that is, not focused on particular goods) trade barriers. But neither are high tariffs a universal prescription for development. Burma and the Socialist Bloc, for example, suffered from isolating themselves behind barriers to trade and international exchanges. Like other economic policies, trade policy is best decided by local authorities, responding to local conditions. They can balance the benefits from building up economic institutions against the costs from attenuated competition.

Keep It Local

The idea that globalization dictates uniform policies on trade, regulation, financial markets, taxation, and the provision of public welfare ignores both the extent to which local economies will determine their own fates and the degree to which persistent, local social and cultural differences call for locally conceived policies in these areas. It is at best misguided and at worst highly destructive to impose uniform economic policies in these areas. Nor is international aid applied with the same generic approach to the broad range of poor nations likely to be more successful. Aid targeted at alleviating specific conditions, like malaria or the lack of adequate drinking water, can be beneficial and significant. But countries that continually depend on the kindness of strangers—Blanche DuBois economic policies—to improve their institutions, their behavior, and their living standards will be gravely disappointed. They should not be given that opportunity.

Chapter 3

Employment Trends for Globalization 3.0

Are All the Good Jobs Going Away?

Fifty years ago, a Kayser-Roth textile mill in Pittsboro, North Carolina, employed 400 workers making hosiery. The mill stopped producing textiles years ago, but the building is still occupied by a company doing manufacturing. Now, 90 workers are using sophisticated and expensive equipment in an effort to extract a drug for liver ailments out of duckweed. The lowest-paid technicians make considerably more than the textile workers ever earned, although there are many fewer of them. If the company succeeds in extracting the drug, its profits will be much higher than those Kayser-Roth achieved from turning out hosiery.[1]

The transformation of this building, from textile mill to biotech facility, illustrates some of the changes in employment within the American economy over those 50 years: a shrinkage of lower-skilled manufacturing jobs, an increase of higher-skilled and better-paid technical jobs, and an anxious concern that the two trends will still leave many workers out in the cold, or at best serving up unhealthful fast foods to an already-obese population.

Recent History as a Guide

Of all the challenges that rampant globalization is thought to pose to economies in the developed world, nothing is more threatening than the loss of good jobs. There are regions in the United States where factory closings have been going on for decades. Even in areas less directly threatened, it is the cloistered person who does not know someone who has lost a job or been forced to take a pay cut, thanks to competition from abroad. For those few who have no direct or secondary experience, the devastating effects of globalization on the American job market are recounted nightly on one national cable news network and somewhat less frequently on the other news programs. So, if attention must be paid to the effects of globalization on employment, no one need fear that it is not getting its due.

Now (in 2008) that we are more than six years into what Thomas Friedman called *Globalization 3.0,* the dire consequences of competition from hundreds of millions of highly productive, low-wage workers in China and India should be visible in the conditions of workers elsewhere. But what the data actually reveal is how little those workers have been affected en masse. Unemployment in the United States stands at around 5 percent, near its historic lows for the period after World War II. Unemployment in Europe is declining. Employment prospects in Japan are improving after more than a decade of stagnation. Wages have not been measurably affected. Previous wage trends in developed countries have either continued or improved slightly. Something else must be at work to counter these gloomy predictions about the consequences of globalization for workers outside of India, China, and a few other developing countries.

We have made two forecasts about the global economy. First, services are likely to be the greatest area of growth, and the majority of these services will be locally produced and locally consumed: housing, medical care, education, legal and social services, recreation, utilities, telecommunications, and others. Second, the future efficiency of individual national economies will be determined locally, not by global developments. Taken together, these two predictions should mean that national economies can control their own fates, and this ability will increase, not diminish, in the future. Well-functioning economies ought to have nothing to fear from China and India.

Nevertheless, a nightmare scenario threatens this positive picture: low-wage, highly productive workers in those countries will be able to produce manufactured goods and provide outsourced services at costs so low that companies and their employees in even the best-functioning national economies will not be able to compete. As production migrates completely to China and India, workers elsewhere will lose their jobs or see their incomes plummet, and labor impoverishment will characterize the rest of the world.

There is a fundamental problem with this doomsday forecast. In a world of flexible exchange rates, the prices that China and India charge for the goods and services they export depend on their costs of production. They pay their workers in Yuan and Rupees. If they run enormous trade surpluses, exporting much more than they import, then the demand for their currencies will vastly exceed the supply. The prices of the currencies will rise, and so will the costs of production. Their exports will be less cheap, relative to goods produced elsewhere, and their competitive positions less invincible. This is the classic process through which trade imbalances are supposed to be contained and reversed until balance is restored between exports from China and India and their imports from the rest of the world.[2] When that happens, production that, in relative terms, is done most efficiently in China and India will locate there, and production more efficiently done elsewhere, again in relative terms, will find its appropriate home elsewhere. Both sides will benefit from this trade, and it will enhance, not undermine, locally determined productivity levels. And David Ricardo, the great nineteenth-century British economist who founded trade theory on the idea of comparative advantage, will rest in peace.[3]

Even if we dismiss the nightmare scenario in which all of the jobs go to China and India, workers in the rest of the world may still suffer substantially after imports and exports are in balance. Exports from China and India may consist of goods and services produced chiefly by low-skilled labor, while their imports may be goods and services produced by highly skilled workers using large amounts of capital. In this case, even trade that is balanced in the aggregate will lead to a significant decline in demand for relatively less-skilled labor in the rest of the world, putting pressure on wages and jobs for those workers. Depending on how big this less-skilled portion of the labor force actually is, the threat to the economic well-being of many workers and whole economies may be considerable.

Fortunately, history can provide some help in predicting just how far these developments may go to undermine the condition of workers in the developed world. First, competition from efficient, relatively low-wage workers in Asia is not unprecedented. For several decades starting in the 1970s, Japan was regarded as a threat to living standards in the United States, a threat no less serious than that from China and India today. Commentators wrote widely and despairingly about the future "de-industrialization" of the United States. The titles of books published during these years reveal the alarm with which the challenge was viewed:

- *Japan as Number One*, 1979, by Ezra Vogel, a sociologist at Harvard University
- *The Reckoning*, 1986, by David Halberstam, a former reporter and the author of books on Vietnam, the automobile industry, the press, sports, and other contemporary topics
- *Trading Places: How We Allowed Japan to Take the Lead*, 1988, by Clyde Prestowitz, a leading trade negotiator for the U.S. government
- *Cracking the Japanese Market: Strategies for Success in the New Global Economy*, 1991, by James Morgan and Jeffrey J. Morgan

Cracking the Japanese Market begins with this ominous warning:

You can pick up a newspaper in virtually any community in America today and read the same story. American business is in crisis: a major company retreats from a competitive industry, another lays off thousands of employees, still another is acquired by a foreign conglomerate. Nearby, other articles tell a different story: a new electronic product from Japan hits American shores, a Japanese company now dominates a critical market, another has passed its U.S. competitors in development of a new technology. The disparity between the two economies is no longer the stuff of drab journals; it makes headlines from Wall Street to Main Street. It can be argued that at no time in its history has the United States faced any greater challenge than that now being posed by Japan. (p. 3)

Knowing how the threat from Japan has played out should give us some sense of what we face today.

Second, mechanization and automation have been a continuing source of competition for low-wage workers, initially in agriculture, then in manufacturing, and more recently in services. Again, understanding how past challenges have affected patterns of employment and wages should provide guidance in anticipating the likely consequences of competition from China and India.

Finally, detailed information is available on the jobs that Americans, as participants in a high-wage, advanced economy, currently hold. We can examine employment on a job-by-job basis and estimate how likely it is that specific occupations will migrate overseas, from the United States and also from Europe, Japan, and other high-wage countries. This kind of fine-grained analysis has been missing from the debate about the effects of globalization on jobs and wages, and its absence has allowed the scaremongers to flourish. The data actually reveal that fears about the havoc from globalization on workers in high-wage economies have been wildly overblown.

Recent Patterns of Employment and Unemployment in the United States

Job creation in the United States since the late 1960s, when foreign competition became a serious issue, has been robust. Around 78.5 million people were employed in 1970. By 1983, at the height of concerns over trade competition with Japan, that figure had grown to almost 101 million. In 2005, it had reached almost 142 million. During 35 years of increasing globalization, employment in the United States actually increased by over 80 percent. The economy created enough jobs to accommodate three groups that entered the labor market in large numbers during this period: the baby-boom generation, immigrants, and women, many more of whom went to work outside the home. Overall participation in the labor force rose steadily from 60.3 percent of the adult population in 1970 to 63.8 percent in 1983 to 66.1 percent in 2005.

Unemployment has fluctuated, as it always does because of business cycles, but there has been no sustained trend. In 1971, 94.6 percent of the labor force was employed (5.4 percent unemployed). In 1983, in the wake of a serious recession, the figures were 92.9 percent employed, and 7.1 percent unemployed. By 2007, the employment rate had recovered to 95.5 percent, reducing unemployment to 4.5 percent.

The unemployment statistics count only those who are unemployed and actively looking for work. If the number of discouraged workers—those so pessimistic about finding an acceptable job that they stop looking—were to rise, they would not be counted among the unemployed, and the unemployment rate would decline. However, alternative measures of unemployment show a similar picture—essentially full employment with no significant increase in unemployment over the last 10 years of full-throttle globalization. In 2007, people who have been unemployed for 15 weeks or more accounted for 1.5 percent of the total labor force, a figure that has not changed in the last 10 years. Discouraged workers represented 0.2 percent of the workforce in 1997; that figure increased to 0.3 percent in 2007. Underemployed workers constitute a final group, people who are working part time not by choice but because they cannot find an acceptable full-time job. In 1997, these workers made up 2.9 percent of the labor force; in 2007, they accounted for 2.8 percent.

To date, there have never been legions of U.S. workers displaced by globalization. Comparing the figures for 2007 with those for 1997, what stands out is how little has changed in the employment/unemployment data, other than the size of the work-force and the total number of jobs.

The Changing Nature of Work

If the rate of unemployment has not changed, can the same be said about the quality of the jobs workers hold? It is certainly true that some good jobs have disappeared. There were a million and a half autoworkers in 1970, well-paid, with good health and retirement benefits, and unionized. Fewer than half of those jobs remained in 2007. But overall, the average quality of jobs has improved markedly over this period. The most rapidly growing job category has been Managerial and Professional employment, which was also the largest single group in 2005.[4] These high-level jobs accounted for almost one-third of all employment. The only category to decline in absolute numbers was Operators, Fabricators, Laborers, and Farmers, largely manual work. High-level, blue-collar craft jobs (Precision Production, Craft, Repair) rose by 51 percent, a healthy increase though less than the overall job growth of 80 percent. Some of the less-skilled blue-collar jobs (Operators, Fabricators, Laborers) clearly morphed into low-level service jobs, which more than doubled in number. However, taken together, service and low-level, blue-collar jobs increased by about one-third, more slowly than high-level blue-collar jobs and far below the rate of overall job growth (Table 3.1). By 2005, more than 60 percent of all jobs fell within the Managerial/Professional and the Technical, Sales, Administrative Support categories. The quality of jobs improved, along with the total number of jobs, throughout the recent era of globalization.

Table 3.1   Occupational Categories in the United States,
1970–2005 (000s)

Job Category	1970	1983	2005	Percent Change (1970–2005)
Managerial, Professional	18,265	23,592	46,278	153.4%
Technical, Sales, Administrative Support	19,732	31,265	39,738	101.4%
Precision Production, Craft, Repair	10,158	12,328	15,325	50.9%
Operators, Fabricators, Laborers Farmers	20,759	19,791	18,717	−9.8%
Service Occupations	9,712	13,857	21,672	123.1%
Total	*78,626*	*100,833*	*141,730*	*80.3%*

SOURCE: *Statistical Abstract of the United States.* Starting in 2005, the government organized the job data into occupational groupings different from those they had previously used. We have reorganized the detailed data for 2005 to conform as closely as possible to the earlier categories.

The Meaning Is in the Details

Breaking down these categories to take a closer look at changes in occupational composition over this period strengthens the conclusion that more people have better jobs. Within the Managerial and Professional group (Table 3.2), the largest single subcategory by far, and one of the fastest growing, is managers and executives.

All of the occupations in this category are high-prestige jobs, even if some of them are better paid than others, and all

Table 3.2   Managerial/Professional Employment in the United States, 1983–2005 (000s)

Job Type	1983	2005	Percent Change (1970–2005)
Managers, executives	10,807	22,700	110.0%
Teachers, librarians	4,368	7,079	62.1%
Nurses, health professionals	1,900	3,740	96.8%
Scientists	820	3,045	271.3%
Writers, artists, entertainers, athletes	1,544	2,644	71.2%
Social, social science workers	1,092	2,457	125.0%
Architects, engineers	1,675	2,429	45.0%
Doctors, dentists	735	1,153	56.9%
Lawyers, judges	651	1,031	58.4%
Total	*23,592*	*46,278*	*96.2%*

SOURCE: *Statistical Abstract of the United States.*

of them grew faster in this period than the overall employment growth rate, which was 41 percent between 1983 and 2005.

Within the next major category, Technical, Sales, and Administrative Support jobs, the shift toward better jobs has been even more pronounced (Table 3.3). The largest subgroup in 2005, sales supervisors and representatives, includes real estate brokers, stockbrokers, and industrial equipment sales reps. It grew faster than the category as a whole. So did the number of jobs for technicians, which consists of higher-level technical support workers like paralegals, computer programmers, and others. Two subcategories that actually declined were secretaries and clerks and financial recordkeepers. The vanishing secretary was the victim of the widespread adoption of personal computers, which, starting in the early 1980s, automated many of these jobs out of existence, despite the overall economic expansion. Outsourcing and offshoring had little or nothing to do with this job shrinkage. Whatever serious effect they may have

Table 3.3   Technical, Sales, Administrative Support Employment in the United States, 1983–2005 (000s)

Job Type	1983	2005	Percent Change (1970–2005)
Sales supervisors, representatives	6,251	9,354	49.6%
Secretaries, clerks	8,182	7,439	−9.1%
Retail sales workers	5,565	7,079	27.2%
Investigators, material handling specialists, others	4,634	7,463	61.0%
Technicians, technical support (health, science, engineering, computer programmers, paralegals)	3,053	4,834	58.3%
Financial recordkeepers	2,525	2,314	−8.4%
Mail, communications clerks	1,055	1,255	19.0%
Total	31,265	39,738	27.1%

SOURCE: *Statistical Abstract of the United States.*

in the future, their impact to date has been limited. The effect of automation is also noticeable in the relatively slow growth in retail sales jobs. Point-of-sales terminals and computerized inventory management have lessened, though certainly not eliminated, the demand for this kind of work. Overall, it is the simple, low-level jobs that have either declined or grown relatively slowly. They are the easiest to automate, and it is automation that has reduced their numbers or their relative growth. Employment growth within the category has been sustained by the increase of higher-level jobs.

Blue-collar employment has experienced the same trends. Between 1983 and 2005, the more highly skilled jobs in the Precision Production, Craft, and Repair category grew faster than the less-skilled jobs in the Operators, Fabricators, Laborers, and Farmers category (Tables 3.4 and 3.5). Within these categories, the jobs that have grown are those that, because they are decentralized, are difficult to automate or to replace with imports. Jobs in factory or factory-like settings have actually declined in number. The craft jobs in construction and in repair—work done onsite—increased relatively rapidly. Precision production jobs, on the other hand, done in factories,

Table 3.4 Precision Production, Craft, Repair Employment in the United States, 1983–2005 (000s)

Job Type	1983	2005	Percent Change (1970–2005)
Construction trades	4,289	6,718	56.6%
Mechanical repair	4,158	5,226	25.7%
Precision production	3,685	3,281	−11.0%
Mining, extractive	196	100	−49.0%
Total	*12,328*	*15,325*	*24.3%*

SOURCE: *Statistical Abstract of the United States.*

Table 3.5 Operators, Fabricators, Laborers, Farmers Employment in the United States, 1983–2005 (000s)

Job Type	1983	2005	Percent Change (1970–2005)
Transportation operators	4,201	5,553	32.2%
Machine operators	7,744	5,217	−32.6%
Handlers, cleaners, helpers, laborers	4,147	4,954	19.5%
Farmers	3,700	2,993	−19.1%
Total	*19,792*	*18,717*	*−5.4%*

SOURCE: *Statistical Abstract of the United States.*

declined. So did the jobs of machine operators, also working in industrial settings. However, jobs of transportation operators, dispersed on their planes, trains, buses, subways, and taxicabs, became more plentiful. The only exception to the generalization that dispersed jobs fared better was farmers, where automation continued its long history of eroding employment in agriculture.

Service employment in nonprofessional/nontechnical jobs has been growing faster than overall employment (Table 3.6). The actual number of jobs involved, even in 2005, is relatively small. For example, the seven million foodservice workers, those famous "burger flippers" who were expected to dominate the labor force, were fewer in number than the more than nine million high-level sales representatives. The seven million figure includes 317,000 chefs and head cooks, 574,000 first-line supervisors, 304,000 bartenders, and only 305,000 combined food preparation and service (that is, fast-food) workers. The 264,000 dishwashers were outnumbered by 1.8 million generic cooks and 1.9 million waiters and waitresses. The whole group together grew more slowly than building-service workers

Table 3.6 Service Occupations Employment in the United States, 1983–2005 (000s)

Job Type	1983	2005	Percent Change (1970–2005)
Food preparation	4,860	7,159	47.3%
Building services	2,736	4,142	51.4%
Personal services	1,870	3,682	96.9%
Health services	1,739	3,002	72.6%
Protective services	1,672	2,810	68.1%
Private household services	980	877	−10.5%
Total	*13,857*	*21,672*	*56.4%*

SOURCE: *Statistical Abstract of the United States.*

(janitors, cleaners), personal-service workers (hairdressers, childcare workers), health services workers (nursing and home health-care aides, dental assistants), and protective services workers (police officers, security guards, correctional officers, firefighters). Many of these jobs are better than the rote factory jobs they have replaced.

In the period since 1983, overall job growth in the United States has been strong, and the jobs created have generally been good ones. Where job losses have occurred, they have been in low-level positions, capable of automation, in both factories and offices. It is the factory losses that have been the main source of concern, in part because the better-paying jobs, like those in the automobile industry, offered some blue-collar workers an entry into middle-class economic status that otherwise

Table 3.7 International Employment and Unemployment, 2000

Country	Employment Composition			Unemployment Rates
	Raw Materials*	Manufacturing	Services	
United States	3.0%	15.8%	81.2%	4.2%
United Kingdom	3.2%	18.8%	78.0%	5.8%
Netherlands	2.9%	22.0%	75.1%	3.2%
Denmark	3.3%	22.4%	74.3%	4.8%
Average	*3.1%*	*19.8%*	*77.2%*	*4.5%*
Germany	4.1%	25.1%	70.8%	10.7%
France	5.0%	24.4%	70.6%	8.4%
Japan	3.6%	26.6%	69.8%	4.7%
Average	*4.2%*	*25.4%*	*70.4%*	*7.9%*

* Includes agriculture.
SOURCES: *Statistical Abstract of the United States; EC Statistical Annual, OECD.*

would not have been so readily available. Those countries that have suffered from chronic high levels of unemployment, such as France and Germany, or stagnation—Japan—have typically had larger manufacturing sectors than the countries with lower unemployment rates.[5] But it would be a mistake to assume, without examination, that globalization was responsible for the losses of jobs even in manufacturing (Table 3.7).

That Giant Sucking Sound Is Coming from . . .

In his campaign for the presidency in 1992, Ross Perot tried to capitalize on an earlier version of globalization phobia by claiming to hear "the giant sucking sound of (U.S.) jobs going to Mexico." Today, that specific fear seems almost quaint in light of the continuing massive movement of Mexican workers to the United States. But even at the time, Perot's charges were off the mark. Between 1980 and 1991, consumption of manufactured goods in the United States rose by 31 percent, adjusted for inflation, while production of manufactures increased by 25 percent (Table 3.8). The excess growth of imports over

Table 3.8 Production and Consumption of Manufactures, 1981–1991

Consumption change	31%
Employment change	−9%
Difference	40%
Globalization portion	6%
Improved productivity	34%
Share of job loss to globalization	15%
Share of job loss to productivity	85%

SOURCE: U.S. Department of Commerce, Bureau of Economic Analysis.

growth of exports caused this 6 percent difference. During the same period, manufacturing employment in the United States dropped by 9 percent. The change in employment (minus 9) was 40 percentage points below the increase in consumption of 31 percent. Six percent of this 40 percent difference in employment was accounted for by the increase in net imports. The remaining 34 percent—by far the larger portion—was due to growth in productivity. But it is harder to make productivity into a demon and run a political campaign against efficiency than to castigate perfidious corporations for moving jobs to Mexico. Even for the autoworkers mentioned earlier, it was productivity that accounted for most of the lost jobs, considerably more than foreign competitors.

The same trends continue today (Table 3.9). Consumption of manufactures continues to rise, employment continues to decline, although now from a lower base, and net imports make up the difference. Productivity still accounts for a larger portion of the job loss than globalization, although the globalization portion is rising. And manufacturing represents a considerably smaller fraction of overall employment in this period than in 1992 or 1980. Also, all the jobs lost in manufacturing have been

Table 3.9 Production and Consumption of Manufactures, 2000–2006

Consumption change	25%
Production change	10%
Change in net imports (globalization portion)	15%
Employment change	−18%
Difference between consumption and employment	43%
Globalization portion	15%
Improved productivity	28%
Share of job loss to globalization	35%
Share of job loss to productivity	65%

SOURCE: Department of Commerce, Bureau of Economic Analysis.

more than offset by the growth in service jobs of relatively high quality.

The experience of lower-level service jobs has been similar to that of manufacturing. The primary culprit for the loss of jobs has been automation, not job movement overseas. Secretaries, clerks, and financial recordkeepers have been replaced by personal computers, not by lower-paid workers in India or China.

But Will the Future Be Different?

Since 2000, there has been minimal detectable change in the composition of job growth. The most rapidly growing categories continue to be Managerial and Professional and Service occupations, followed by Technical, Sales, Administrative Support and, surprising as it may seem, high-level blue-collar jobs. Lower-level manual jobs, in the Operator/Fabricator/Laborer/Farmer category, have not increased at all. What has not declined are the fears about the potential for accelerated job losses through outsourcing and offshoring.

The recent history of changes in employment categories and job types (Tables 3.1–3.6) should allay some of those fears. The characteristics of some of these jobs make it difficult, if not impossible, for them to be shipped abroad, no matter how fast the communication links nor how cheap the transportation becomes.

Managerial and professional occupations are not very vulnerable. Management and executive jobs, by their very nature, cannot be offshored. They depend on direct interaction between managers and employees. Dispersed service activities are likely to continue to grow, and they need to be performed onsite. As discussed in Chapter 1, education is not going to be provided remotely, at least not in large scale or in the foreseeable future.

Thus, jobs for teachers and librarians are not threatened by globalization. Lawyers and judges, doctors and dentists, social and social science workers, and nurses and other health professionals are also not likely to be threatened by offshoring. Scientists, engineers, and architects might be more vulnerable to outsourcing and offshoring, at least in theory. In practice, the importance of close relationships between research and implementation and the benefits of concentrated research communities like Silicon Valley, which are currently located disproportionately in the United States and elsewhere in the developed world, mean that these activities are going to be difficult to move overseas.

Writers, artists, entertainers, and athletes make up about 2.6 million of over 46 million Managerial and Professional jobs. Within that 2.6 million, there are 273,000 athletes, coaches, umpires, and related workers, 150,000 photographers, 213,000 musicians and singers, 100,000 public relations specialists (the census had to put them somewhere), and 92,000 broadcast technicians. These and similar jobs are not subject to outsourcing, although professional athletes may be imported in increasing numbers, at least during the season. The roughly one million designers and writers are unlikely to find themselves out of work because Indian or Chinese designers or writers are doing their jobs for less, so long as cultural preference remain important. Automation and domestic Internet-enabled decentralization are likely to pose more of a threat to these workers than globalization.

The Managerial and Professional category as a whole is not very threatened by globalization and, anecdotal evidence aside, serious studies of outsourcing and offshoring do not anticipate substantial job losses in this category any time soon.

Service and craft occupations are also secure. Food preparation, building services, personal services, protective services, and private household services are all tethered to their local venues.

Service occupations in health care, like practical nursing, must also be done locally. None of these jobs can be effectively offshored, which explains why they are a magnet for immigrants, both legal and illegal, to the United States.

Craft jobs today are largely in construction and repair services, such as plumbing. They need to be done onsite. Precision jobs within factories accounts for about 20 percent of the job category. They are more threatened by automation than offshoring. Job losses here are likely to be offset by gains in construction and repair, which account for the recent employment growth in the Craft category.

Low-level blue-collar jobs are largely safe from further erosion due to cheap imports. Transportation, distribution, construction, and agriculture accounts for about 70 percent of these jobs, and all of them must be done locally. The other 30 percent, or roughly 5 million jobs, are in manufacturing. As we have demonstrated, they are more threatened by automation—productivity improvements—than by globalization. Also, they are not great jobs by almost any standard, and any losses here will be more than offset by growth in lower-level service jobs.

The remaining category, Technical, Sales, Administrative Support, is the most vulnerable to moving overseas. Some higher-level sales jobs, like real estate brokers, depend on direct personal contact and the need to show local property. Others, like stockbrokers, may have lost positions to automation, but most brokers will remain because clients are more comfortable with direct and continued contact with a person they know and trust for the high-value transactions involved. Retail sales clerks, investigators, and people involved in material distribution must also do their jobs locally. Technicians who work on or with physical materials, like specimens and laboratory equipment, also need to be in close proximity to the professionals they support. The vulnerable jobs are limited chiefly to computer

programming (581,000 jobs), clerical work, and records processing, especially those that entail work over the telephone or
the Internet. These jobs have been under siege for years from
computer-based automation, and their number has been declining without impairing the overall growth rate of employment.
For workers in developed countries, these are not, except for
computer programming, "good" jobs, and the decline here will
be more than offset by growth in comparable jobs elsewhere in
the service sector.

This fine-grained look at the work that Americans currently
do, and which European and Japanese workers are increasingly
doing, should calm the fear that many jobs, especially "good"
jobs, are about to disappear overseas. When someone like economist Alan Blinder claims that 40 million jobs in the United
States may be lost overseas, it is not at all clear which jobs he
has in mind.[6] Jobs are always being lost to automation and productivity growth, but the overall employment figures have been
strong, and that pattern is likely to continue. The jobs most
likely to migrate overseas are generally those that can be made
routine and thus automated. With the advent of personal computing power since the early 1980s, we have already witnessed
this process at work and the displacement that it causes. But the
consequences have not been severe for employment growth or
for wage levels, which is what we look at next.

What about Wages?

Most people work to get paid, and low levels of unemployment
are less commendable if real wages are actually declining or not
keeping up with growth in national income. In fact, wage trends
have lagged behind overall economic and employment growth.
One reason is the growth of the labor force. The baby-boom

generation, the increase in the number and percentage of women holding jobs outside the home, and legal and illegal immigration on a large scale have all expanded the supply of labor, which should exert downward pressure on wages. In Europe and in Japan, where the labor force has grown less rapidly, wages have risen more than in the United States, even as employment growth has been slower and unemployment generally higher. Still, the relatively slow growth of wages in the United States has been an unwelcome development, especially given recent increases in productivity growth. How much of the shortfall in this trend is due to globalization, how much to other changes shaping the economy?

The standard definition of *wages* is the average hourly earnings of private, nonsupervisory workers. This group excludes managers (supervisory) and professionals, people who have done relatively well in the recent past and now make up the largest group of workers. That exclusion is appropriate because concern over the impact of globalization is not about its effect on well-off, highly qualified employees, but about the damage it is thought to be doing to the average worker. Also, there is a distinction between earnings and total compensation, which includes the cost of fringe benefits like medical insurance, employer pension contributions, workman's compensation premiums, and government-provided unemployment insurance. Reported average hourly earnings do not include fringe benefits. As the cost of these benefits has increased, especially for medical insurance, the gap between earnings and total compensation has also widened.

For example, between 1982 and 2000, average hourly real (adjusted for inflation) wages grew by only 2.3 percent, according to Bureau of Labor statistics. During the same period, total real compensation increased by 19.9 percent. Between 2000 and 2006, real wages grew by 2.7 percent and total real compensation by 6.4 percent. In discussions about what globalization is doing to income, the most frequently cited figure is real wages. It is the one we will use. However, because it excludes both supervisory workers and fringe benefits, trends in real wages tend to understate aggregate average improvements in standards of living. Since this trend has coincided with the recent intensification of globalization, globalization has been blamed for the meager rise in real wages. But because the real wage figures are an increasingly unreliable measure of economic well-being, they represent the worst case of the harm that can be attributed to globalization.

Over the 13 years between 1970 and 1982, when manufacturing in the United States first faced serious foreign competition, wages actually fell by 6 percent in real terms (Table 3.10). During the next 17 years, from 1983 to 2000, wages were essentially unchanged, rising by just 1 percent. Since 2000, in the era of Globalization 3.0, wages have actually risen by 2.7 percent. Any negative impact of globalization on real wages appears to be diminishing, not accelerating. In the six years starting in 1977, real wages fell by 8.2 percent, which was worse by 11 percent than the experience of 2000 to 2006. The economy in 1977 had a higher percentage of employees working in manufacturing, and they no doubt took the brunt

Table 3.10   Changes in Real Average Hourly Earnings (Private, Nonsupervisory Workers)

Period	Change (Total for Period)
1970–1983	−6.0%
1983–2000	1.0%
2000–2006	2.7%

SOURCE: Bureau of Labor Statistics.

of the hit from the Japanese imports. The negative impact of globalization on wages is old, not current, news.[7] The effects of globalization on wages may have been significant in the past, but they have been moderated by the shift in employment toward service jobs, which are far less vulnerable to foreign competition than those in manufacturing. As this trend continues, it is unlikely that things will get worse in the future.

Chapter 4

Can We Make Any Money?

What Globalization Does to Profits

At his confirmation hearings in 1953 to be Secretary of Defense, Charles Wilson, CEO of General Motors, said, ". . . for years I thought what was good for the country was good for General Motors and vice versa." The issue was whether he should sell his stock in the company in order to avoid a conflict of interest. Wilson did sell the stock, and depending on how he reinvested the proceeds, the Senate Armed Services Committee may have done him and especially his heirs a great service.

Putting aside the returns on their investment, it does seem clear in the twenty-first century that what is bad for GM may not be so bad for the country, and that the once-tightly intertwined interests of the automobile giant and the rest of America have been weakened, if not entirely eliminated. The larger issue is the extent to which globalization has changed the terms under which companies compete with one another, and whether profitability is as dated as the tail fins on a 1958 Cadillac. To give the answer away, globalization has not repealed the underlying rules of market economies. Firms that operate in intensely competitive industries will not get very rich. Those fortunate companies that have markets to themselves—with perhaps a few friendly competitors—will continue to thrive.

Companies Under Globalization 3.0

The current round of globalization has not curtailed economic growth in the developed world. Although employees in certain industries have been hurt, workers in general have not suffered in any major way as economies have become more open. What about businesses, the other main component of national income? Have profits been undermined by intensified competition from foreign firms? Or, conversely, has globalization presented opportunities for the strongest firms to expand both their revenues and their incomes in the larger markets now open to them?

In a previous period of severe globalization anxiety, in the later 1970s and 1980s, even established giants like GM, Ford, Volkswagen, RCA, and Philips were rocked by powerful new Asian competitors such as Toyota, Honda, Sony, and Mitsubishi. Profits shrank; for some of these companies, they have never really recovered. The S&P 500 index is the most widely used barometer for the U.S. stock market. In the 10 years ending in August 1982, it had been stationary, moving down a point from 104 to 103 (and, since dividends are included in that index number, the return was considerably worse). In the 10 years ending in December 2007, the index rose from 970 to 1,468. The path was hardly smooth. The collapse of the Internet bubble and the recession of 2001 took their toll, as both earnings and share prices declined for several years. But the earnings of the companies grew from $38 per index unit in 1998 to $66 in 2007. If Globalization 3.0 is making it more difficult for companies to earn a profit, that fact has yet to show up in the data.[1]

Some iconic U.S. companies have become endangered again. Ford and GM are once more under threat. But this time the culprits are not any new corporate heavyweights from China or India. They are the well-established European and Japanese competitors, plus rising oil prices and the inexorable growth of retiree medical costs. New developments in globalization are not a factor. One notable difference in this current round is the absence of powerful new global corporate players. The biggest Chinese companies are not ones that threaten to dominate global markets. Some are oil companies that exploit local natural resources. Others are local power and telecommunications utilities. Still others are local Chinese banks, financial institutions, and construction companies. Even the industrial companies, like Sinochem and Baosteel, produce largely for local Chinese markets. The few manufacturing firms within China's largest 25 companies, like China FAW Group, which makes auto parts, and Shanghai Automotive, are small relative to their global competitors, and they are strikingly unprofitable. Shanghai Automotive reports a return on equity of under 2 percent; China FAW is slightly better, at 3.5 percent. The Chinese companies with effective global operations consist chiefly of surviving Hong Kong enterprises, such as Hutchinson Whampoa and Jardine Matheson.

If major western businesses are threatened by the current round of globalization, it is not by emergent Chinese corporate giants.

A few Indian companies have been more visible. Technology outsourcing firms like Infosys and Wipro are repeatedly invoked to illustrate the threat that globalization presents even to highly skilled workers. Unlike the large Chinese enterprises, these companies are profitable and growing rapidly. But in the broad scheme of things, they are surprisingly small. In 2007, Wipro had a market capitalization of $20 billion, not tiny by any means, but it was based on revenues of $3.7 billion for 2006–2007, of which $2.5 billion were global IT sales. Net income was just over $700 million. Infosys is around the same size. For all the attention they have attracted, these companies are hardly likely to undermine the enterprises that make up either the U.S. economy, with a GDP of $13 trillion, the comparably sized economy of the European Community, or that of Japan, at around $4.5 trillion.

The other side of this story is the healthy earnings of companies in the developed world. In the United States, corporate profits as a share of national income have risen steadily, from 8.6 percent in 1990 to 9.3 percent in 2000 to 13.3 percent in 2006. Proprietors' income, the return to small, unincorporated businesses, has also risen, from 7.5 percent in 1990 to 8.3 percent in 2000 and to 8.6 percent in 2006.[2] In Europe, after a long decline, profits including proprietors' income have increased as a share of national income. For the core 25 countries in the European Union, profits as a fraction of national income grew from 37.6 percent in 2000 to 38.8 percent in 2006. They are now about the same or slightly above profit levels in the mid 1990s, before the advent of this round of globalization anxiety. Japan shows a similar pattern, a slight increase from 18.3 percent of national income in 2000 to 19.1 percent in 2005, the latest years for which comprehensive Japanese figures are available.[3] Clearly, the current data do not support the bleak picture of a new global world dominated by relentless competition from foreign firms exploiting hundreds of millions of educated, highly efficient, yet low-wage workers in India and China.

Perhaps globalization has been an opportunity, rather than a threat. After all, economies of scale might become more potent with the world as a market, and the ability to reproduce successful and efficient business models across the world could usher in a golden age of global profitability for established companies in the developed world. However, just as the fear that globalization will eliminate profits has not been supported by events, so, too, the hope that firms will thrive through global expansion has not been realized.

The international expansion of Wal-Mart provides a useful cautionary example. Wal-Mart is the very model of a potential global behemoth. With sales of more than $300 billion, it dwarfs all other retailers. Its global purchasing power is legendary. Its operations are renowned for their efficiency. It has made the concept of *supply chain* almost sexy. Wal-Mart's sales tracking, inventory management, and logistics systems are exemplars for the retail industry and for any company or organization, such as the military, that has to operate on an enormous scale. Its information technology is cutting edge. The management of its stores and a labor force of more than one million is studied by others within the industry and outside. Wal-Mart is such a model of efficiency that the supposedly unsophisticated traditional retailers of Europe, Asia, and the developing countries should be unable to compete, once Wal-Mart is permitted to enter their markets.

But going abroad has not worked out well for Wal-Mart. In most of the rest of the world, its operations are either losing money or are barely profitable. It has already closed up shop in South Korea and Germany. In England, Wal-Mart bought its way into the market by buying ASDA, regarded as Britain's most efficient retailer. It has not been able to improve on ASDA's performance to any significant extent. Only in Mexico and Canada, which are contiguous to Wal-Mart's core U.S. market, has the company been clearly successful. If even Wal-Mart has been unable to take significant advantage of global opportunities, then perhaps those opportunities may be less available than proponents of globalization assert.

What impact globalization will have on corporate profitability and how companies can respond successfully to globalization are very much open questions. To answer them requires more than anecdotes about the success or failure of a few visible firms, and more than some quantitative evidence from the first few years of Globalization 3.0. We also need some general understanding of how company profitability is determined in a dynamic and competitive market environment. Only then can we think realistically about how companies are likely to be affected by globalization and how they can best respond to challenges and opportunities.

Why Some Companies Are Profitable

The profits that a business earns and that sustain its ongoing operations and fund its growth have traditionally been viewed as an appropriate return on the use of the capital employed, relative to the risks to which the capital is exposed, and as payment for the otherwise uncompensated efforts of the managers and owners of the business. In a competitive environment, a business in which there is no capital involved, and therefore no capital at risk, cannot be expected to earn any return beyond what is justified by the time, energy, and skill of its owner/ managers. If profits exceed that amount, other managers will enter the market—no capital required—and the increase in competition will either drive down prices, reduce the volume of sales for existing firms, or both. Profit margins will drop, as will earnings. As long as there is nothing to prevent new competitors from entering this market, they will continue to flood in, provided they can earn any profit at all, meaning a return in excess of a fair wage for their time and effort. In the long run, average profits will be driven to zero. Without capital investments, competitive markets should not yield significant profits.

The situation is only slightly different when a business does require capital investment, whether for equipment, buildings, inventories, product development, employee training, customer acquisition, or any other asset or expense that cannot be paid for out of current cash flows. The return on that capital—the profit of the business—is determined by a similar competitive process. Say investors are willing to commit capital for a 10 percent return, which presumably compensates them for the risks involved added to the return they could earn on a risk-free investment like Treasury bills. If the business needs $100 million in capital, then over time profits will be driven toward $10 million, the return of 10 percent on $100 million. If it earns more, say $20 million, then other firms will raise capital at 10 percent and compete for a share of that extra return. With competition made more intense by the new entrants, margins will shrink and the profits continue to fall until they have been driven down to the 10 percent return on capital. At that point, no newcomers will be attracted because extra returns are no longer available. As long as nothing stops newcomers from flocking into the industry, as long, in other words, as there are no barriers to entry, this process will be inexorable, and economic profits—profits above what it costs to attract the necessary capital—will not be sustainable.

The process may proceed too far, and competition may reduce returns to $5 million on each $100 million invested. At that point, the investment process goes into reverse: No additional capital will be available, assets will wear out or become obsolete, no new products will be introduced, output will decline, capacity will shrink, and some firms will exit the market, either voluntarily or through failure. After a while, unless demand has dried up, the remaining firms will be able to raise prices and see their profit margins improve. The return on capital will move back toward the 10 percent that investors require. In this self-correcting process, the exit/shrinkage period is more painful and takes longer to accomplish than the new entrant/expansion phase. Assets take time to wear out, and investors' capital may be captive to self-serving managers who persist in reinvesting whatever meager earnings there are, at low rates of return. But over time, the lack of new investment and the shrinkage of production will raise profitability until it gets back up to normal, which in this example is 10 percent on invested capital.

Profits in Competitive Markets: Low Before Globalization, and Low After

The dynamics of competitive markets are familiar. These are the markets in which commodity businesses compete. Because commodities are essentially interchangeable, customers have no loyalty to any supplier. They will switch to whichever supplier is offering better terms. In these competitive situations, average returns will be driven toward the cost of capital, or 10 percent in our example, but it is highly unlikely that every firm will earn that return. Efficient newcomers may drive out less efficient, established competitors. Prevailing prices will be set by the efficient firms, and the others, unable to charge more, will have to settle for lower returns. And these competitive conditions apply in markets for products that are not genuine commodities, like tennis balls or personal computers. As long as buyers can be easily induced to substitute one product for another—if

Dunlops are on sale, do we still buy Wilsons?—the competitive pressures are relentless.

The threat from globalization is easily understood in this kind of market. Efficient Chinese, Indian, or other Asian firms able to employ low-wage, high-quality workers will set prices that even the best operators in high-wage economies will have difficulty matching. Returns on invested capital for these companies will be inadequate, and over time they will be driven from the industries in question. This is the most prevalent globalization scenario, but it ignores several important elements of the actual situation.

First, not all the activities within a particular business are equally subject to global competition. Take sneakers as an example. They are not a pure commodity product; there is some differentiation in styling, technology, and image. But customers are hardly wedded to one brand, so prices can't get too far out of line. Most of the sneakers available today are manufactured in China or some other low-wage Asian country. Still, design, marketing, advertising, and distribution are either wholly or largely done locally. Advertising and distribution have to be located where the customers are. For design, local tastes still differ substantially and need to be satisfied by knowledgeable professionals. The only function that is footloose is manufacturing, and it will gravitate to the low-cost-with-high-quality location. But many products can be made using highly automated processes for which low-cost labor may be less of an advantage than proximity to target markets. So not all the capital employed, even in manufacturing or in commodity markets, is subject to competition from global manufacturers that produce in low-wage Asian countries.

Even some true commodity products that are expensive to transport relative to their price—like cement, wallboard, and construction beams—are relatively immune from global competition. So are other traditional commodities, including metals, agricultural products, coal, oil, and timber. There are at least three reasons. First, these industries are highly automated and use small numbers of relatively skilled workers. As we saw in Chapter 3, there are few Americans working in farming and extractive industries.

Second, and more important, true commodity businesses like petroleum production rely on the combination of labor, capital, and local resource endowments—accessible oil, coal, and mineral deposits, or suitable agricultural land. They can't be moved to low-wage countries, which is why most oil still comes from the Middle East or Russia, regardless of developments in India or China. The advantages conveyed by these endowments are by definition local in nature, and benefit their local owners and providers of the local capital used in their extraction. These businesses are not likely to be adversely affected by future globalization. To the extent that increases in international trade encourage economic growth, increasing demand for these commodities will likely only make their local owners even richer.

Third, commodity and quasi-commodity businesses have been notorious for intense competition and, naturally, low profits. The manufacture of toys, trinkets, small appliances, consumer electronics, standard clothing, shoes, household hardware, and the like has not been a source of significant profits for many years. In these industries, competition from firms in Japan, South Korea, Thailand, and a host of other countries is old news. The few firms still remaining in the United States and other developed countries have survived by focusing on extensive automation and high-quality products, but their profits from manufacturing have not been large for many years. The recently heightened Asian competition is part of a continuing and familiar story. The imbalance between U.S. imports and exports has been increasing steadily since the early 1970s, and businesses have been coping with the challenges of this competition for many years.

On the other side of the Pacific, the manufacturers that have been using low-wage labor to supply U.S. and other developed-country markets have not been immune from the rigors of competitive commodity markets. Firms in India and China have to compete with other low-cost producers in their home countries, and as increasing demand raises the price of labor, they have to fend off manufacturers in Vietnam, Thailand, and other Asian countries, where labor costs are even lower than in theirs. In this environment, less efficient firms are driven to the wall, just as they have been in the developed countries. Even the most efficient companies in China and India will find their profits under constant competitive pressure. "Commodity" competition is an equal-opportunity destroyer of business profitability.

Finally, the capital invested in these businesses is mobile. Over time, the business functions and the capital investments that support them will migrate to the locations where they can be carried out most efficiently, and therefore most profitably. In the sneaker example, the manufacturing takes place where the labor is low-cost but sufficiently skilled, while design, marketing, advertising, and distribution occur in the place where the sneakers are going to be sold. Pharmaceutical companies will do their basic research in areas with access to the world's leading centers of biomedical research and with the amenities that attract highly skilled researchers. Clinical trials and marketing efforts will be concentrated predominantly in areas where the drugs will be sold and, thus, where they must gain acceptance by local medical establishments. Manufacturing will locate where, for tax or other reasons, the costs are lowest. The capital employed in each of these functions of the pharmaceutical company's business will migrate to the location where its return is highest. In this process, the overall returns to the company will be affected only slightly, if at all, by emerging global competition.[4]

The fact that profitability in commodity and quasi-commodity businesses does not appear to have suffered significantly from globalization ought not to be a surprise. These businesses, natural resources aside, were competitive to begin with, and they remain so. Many of them, especially in services, are largely immune to global competition. Some, such as dry cleaners, face only local competition. Others, such as Nike, are adept at operating in a global environment, transferring capital to the locations where its yield is highest. Natural resource industries may actually benefit from globalization as rapid output growth in Asia creates relative resource scarcities and higher resource prices. Overall, the absence of highly profitable Chinese and Indian manufacturing businesses and the favorable profit trends in developed-country returns, described earlier, are likely to continue.

Profits in Protected Markets: Do They Survive?

So far, we have concentrated on businesses in industries and markets without significant barriers to new entry from competitors, including global competitors. They are not the only kind. Some companies, Coca-Cola being a good example, have historically earned annual returns on invested capital of well over 20 percent, which is a lot more than the cost of capital to them. Their stock trades for much more than the value of the net assets used in the business. Yet these returns, far in excess of what it would cost for a competitor to enter the business, have not been undermined by new entrants into their markets. Is that situation going to change in a global economy? Are these companies going to find their protected market positions disappearing? Or does globalization offer them lucrative opportunities to expand their profitable businesses into international markets?

History has not been kind to some of these types of companies. Consider the case of General Motors. From the 1930s to the 1960s, it dominated the domestic U.S. automobile market. Its average pretax return on capital was 45 percent in the 1960s, on a par with Coca-Cola. But in the 1970s, its position and its profitability began to erode as Japanese and European companies entered the U.S. market. Its average pretax return on invested capital fell to 28 percent in the 1970s, down substantially but still far above the cost of capital. GM's situation worsened in the next two decades. Any barriers to entry that had protected it before appear to have largely disappeared, as Japanese and European cars flooded the U.S. market. The average pretax return in the 1980s was 8 percent, and that dropped to 6 percent in the 1990s. It has not turned around in the new century. GM's is a cautionary tale about the impact of globalization in a previous era.

Why has it succumbed to competition when Coca-Cola has not? Product differentiation and branding, often cited as a strategy for coping with competition, are not the answer here. GM's products are as differentiated and branded as Coke's. Clearly, brands were not sufficient to guarantee profits. In the newspaper industry, famous names such as the *New York Times*, the *Wall Street Journal*, and *USA Today* have been far less profitable, and less able to withstand the challenge from electronic media delivered over the Internet, than obscure local newspapers like the *Buffalo Evening News* or various Gannett papers. Brands with reputations for high quality, such as Mercedes-Benz, Sony, and Maytag, have fared less well than more prosaic brands like Tide detergent or Colgate toothpaste. Glamorous industries such as fashion apparel and cosmetics, with many high-profile brands, are often far less profitable than humdrum industries such as insurance or waste management. In financial services, prominent national banks such as Citicorp, Bank of America, and JPMorgan Chase are generally less profitable than smaller banks with lower profiles but strong local presences. Even Coca-Cola is a lot less prestigious than Mercedes-Benz, and a lot more profitable. Product differentiation and branding are not, by themselves, guarantors of profitability.

Competition between branded products takes a different form than among commodities, where competitors keep lowering prices—nothing else differentiates one bushel of spring wheat from another—until only the most efficient are earning anything. When Mercedes competes against Cadillac, it does not try to undercut it on price. Both companies have considerable latitude in what they can charge. Still, if they earn excess returns on the capital invested in their business, they attract new competitors such as Toyota with Lexus and Nissan with Infiniti, which jump in to claim a part of the spoils. And the competition among this expanded roster of luxury brands will undermine profits. The companies may not cut their prices, but they will lose some of their sales to the new entrants. With fewer units sold, the fixed cost per unit—the costs they incur regardless of their volume of sales—will have to go up. It is expensive to support differentiated luxury products. In this case, there are the costs of product development, advertising, and extensive dealer and service networks. Unless they can raise their prices, which is not likely because of the increased competition, the companies will see their fixed costs per unit rise and their profit margins shrink. Lower profit margins on fewer sales is hardly a blueprint for success. Overall profits decline, as do returns on invested capital.

Despite their differentiated products, it turns out that luxury car makers are subject to the same competitive pressures as wheat farmers—new entrants will shrink profits. The form of the competition is a bit different. Instead of the lower prices that confront producers in commodity markets, the luxury car makers were done in by fewer sales and higher unit costs. But the bottom line, literally, is the same.

Sustained protection from the intense competition that shrinks profits to no more than the cost of capital requires something that will keep potential new entrants from deciding to join in. In the language of economics, it requires *barriers to entry*. Product differentiation, by itself, does not qualify as a barrier. It did not protect Cadillac and Lincoln. On the other hand, there is something about Coca-Cola that has kept it more or less immune from the competitive forces that undermined GM. The key to the ongoing profitability of companies such as Coca-Cola is the extent to which existing barriers to entry will survive in a world of increasing globalization.

How to Keep Competitors Out

Before the era of deregulation and more open international trade, the most powerful and obvious barriers to entry were government laws and regulations: licensing laws; preferential treatment of established companies through contracts, franchises, or other favors; and tariffs and import quotas. These state-administered protections are increasingly rare. Established businesses are finding themselves competing with new entrants on playing fields that are officially more level. With less government interference, sustainable barriers to entry must be based on the underlying economic situation of incumbent firms. Established firms must possess economic advantages that potential entrants cannot match.

These competitive advantages are the source of the barriers to entry that allow incumbent firms to sustain high levels of profitability, which would disappear if newcomers could compete on even terms. Anyone who wants to make an informed estimate of how companies like Coca-Cola will perform under the pressure of increasing global competition has to understand the nature of its competitive advantages and how these advantages will hold up in this ostensibly new environment. The same understanding ought to guide the Coca-Colas of the world in responding to that pressure.

Lower Costs

Lower costs are an obvious source of competitive advantage. An incumbent firm may deter newcomers from entering because they cannot match its low-cost structure. Its cost advantages may come either from access to resources on advantageous terms—cheap labor, low-cost capital, or special skills—or because it has proprietary technology that allows it to produce more efficiently than anyone else. The advantage from better access to resources is rare, generally short-lived, and uncertain. Some companies will indeed be smarter than some of their rivals, quicker to seize new opportunities, less bureaucratic, and more entrepreneurial. They may benefit because their competitors have a unionized workforce and they do not. However, the rivals that matter are not the slowest and highest-cost ones, but the most efficient. Intelligence is the property of individuals, not companies, and is available to rivals on equal terms in a competitive labor market. The same thing is true of nonunion labor; if one company in an industry can avoid the unions, so can others. There is nothing about entrepreneurial talents, special skills, or inexpensive labor that can give incumbents any lasting advantage over potential entrants into their markets. The same resources are available to all.

Special access to capital is another illusive competitive advantage. This access is thought to come in two forms. There are companies with "deep pockets," meaning strong balance sheets and borrowing capacity that potential competitors cannot match. But however deep General Motors' pockets, the other automobile companies, both foreign and domestic, had no trouble coming up with the capital they needed to compete. IBM had deep pockets, but that did not keep Microsoft and Intel from winning the lion's share of profits in the personal computer industry and ending up with pockets as deep or deeper than IBM. AT&T was enormously rich when it decided to enter the data-processing market, but it found that the whole industry was populated with companies that also had plenty of assets. The world is awash in large, well-financed business enterprises with deep pockets. And if they do not already exist, the Internet-bubble era in the stock market indicates how easily they can be created with external financing. The lesson from history is that companies such as AT&T, which rely on deep pockets to give them an edge, are more likely to end up with shallower pockets than with permanent competitive advantages.

A second version of the low-cost capital advantage highlights the company that, for historical reasons, has access to capital that looks cheap. It may have issued bonds when interest rates were low and so pays less in debt service than a firm with bonds issued with a higher coupon. But this advantage is also specious. Even if its bonds pay out only 2 percent in interest, the company's true cost of capital—the opportunity cost—is set by the highest return it can earn on that money. If it can earn 8 percent by buying the bonds of other companies, then investing its funds on internal operations that earn less than 8 percent is simply stupid. Stupidity is rarely a competitive advantage.

Certain specialized assets acquired on favorable terms can provide a long-term benefit. Retailers who have favorable leases at desirable locations can benefit, as can companies that own natural resources such as mineral deposits, bought at prices substantially below the current market level. Though these advantages are real, they are by their very nature rare and relatively fleeting. Leases expire; minerals and other resources are ultimately exhausted. And neither can be replaced at anything below current price levels.

Most durable cost advantages arise from proprietary technologies. These technologies may be related to products, like pharmaceuticals, or to processes, like the ability to manufacture chemicals or microprocessors more cheaply. They may be protected legally by patents or be embedded in complex operations whose full dimensions are difficult for outsiders to reproduce. These skill-based advantages can be dynamic, as firms with experience in particular processes or products maintain their lead even as technologies change. Because they turn out more units, they move down the learning curve faster than later entrants and so continue to produce at lower costs and capture more business.

More Demand

Advantages on the demand side complement the supply advantages that stem from lower costs. An incumbent firm may be able to fend off challengers because its customers, of whom it has many, are loyal and not easily seduced away by a newcomer. A company earning a high return on capital can be protected from potential entrants that realize they will have a difficult time attracting enough customers to become profitable. Customers are in a sense captive to the firms that supply the products and services they prefer. It is loyalty to the brand that creates barriers to entry, not the brand image by itself.

The source of the loyalty may be habit, the costs of switching to another supplier, or the difficulties of searching for an acceptable alternative. Loyalty based on habit occurs when purchases are frequent and when customers want a uniform experience from one purchase to the next. Coca-Cola, or Pepsi for its fans, Colgate or Crest toothpaste, Tide or All detergent, Marlboro or Winston cigarettes—each of these brands has customers who are loyal by reflex. This kind of reflexive loyalty is somewhat fortuitous for the company whose products command it. It doesn't apply with the same tenacity to beer drinkers, who will order a Mexican beer in a Mexican restaurant—the Coke lover does not order Montezuma Cola, perhaps because it doesn't exist—or a Japanese beer in a Japanese restaurant, despite their attachment to Budweiser in the supermarket.

Switching costs keep customers tied to products or services that require learning, setup time, or other complex involvement. Microsoft's Windows operating system, for example, has customers firmly attached both because switching to an alternative would require extensive retraining of the current users, and also because customers would have to buy new applications software—and then learn to use that—to integrate with another operating system. Banks have a grasp on customers because changing to another bank is time-consuming, especially when paycheck-deposit and bill-paying arrangements are in place. It is possible to drive current customers away with really dreadful service, but otherwise continuity rates are high.

The third source of customer captivity is search costs. To replace Corn Flakes with Cheerios as your kids' cereal of choice is easy, provided they go along. But changing doctors, lawyers, accountants, or financial advisors is not so simple. More is at stake, and it takes time and effort to examine the alternatives and gain confidence that they will serve at least as well as the incumbents. So habit, switching costs, and search costs all work to attach customers to their current suppliers, and customer captivity (demand) advantages is the second competitive advantage, along with lower costs (supply) advantages, that keeps competitors from flocking into lucrative markets for a share of the high returns.

Economies of Scale

There is a third competitive advantage that may be the most significant and durable of the group. Economies of scale come into play when fixed costs make up a significant part of the total costs of producing the product or service. In the case of Coca-Cola, the fixed costs include advertising, its sales force, and distribution infrastructure, the warehouses and trucks it takes to get the soda to stores, restaurants, and other users. These costs do not rise or fall, at least in the short and medium term, with the level of sales. Any potential competitor that wants to go head-to-head with Coke will have to spend an equivalent amount, but since its sales volume will be considerably lower, the fixed cost per unit sold will be much higher. Coca-Cola's total costs per unit will be significantly lower, thanks to these economies of scale, even without proprietary technology. Entrants with small unit volumes will have high unit costs; at a competitive price, they won't make any money. If they try to attract customers by lowering prices, the incumbent can match them and still have higher margins. In fact, the incumbent can welcome the newcomer by initiating the lower pricing, just to make sure that the entrant is losing money. Unless they are somehow blind to these easily understood facts or believe that they will attract customers so quickly that they approach the scale of the incumbent, potential entrants will be deterred from entering, even though the incumbent is highly profitable.

Network externalities are a variety of ordinary economies of scale. eBay, which dominates the online auction market, is a prime example of companies that profit from network externalities. Buyers are attracted because there are so many items for sale, and sellers are attracted because there are so many buyers. An entrant cannot hope to succeed by attracting buyers and sellers a handful at a time; they will stay with eBay because of its reach. In this case, the size of its operation is a crucial component of eBay's appeal, which only grows as the market itself expands. For eBay, this is a virtuous circle. For any would-be competitor, it is an effective barrier to entry.

In both versions of economies of scale, the incumbent must keep its size lead over any competitor in order to maintain its cost advantage. Two conditions are necessary. First, there has to be some degree of customer captivity, or at least inertia. If the newcomer has equal access to customers, meaning that customers have no attachment to the incumbent, then every day brings new and equal competition for business. If the customers divide more or less evenly among the companies, all economies of scale advantages disappear since each can spread the fixed costs over the same volume of sales. Entrants who can compete on quality, price, features, and other things customers want will be playing on a level field with the incumbent. Since each will have roughly the same volume of sales, each will reach the same scale of operations and same cost per unit. None of the advantages that come from economies of scale can survive if competitors can achieve the same scale of operation. With its customers bound to it by habit, Coca-Cola has been able to benefit from an economies of scale advantage over many years, and in many places.

The second condition essential for an economies of scale advantage to persist relates to the size of the market in which the incumbent operates. If the market is very large, then a new entrant may win enough business to realize the benefits of scale even if it captures only a small market share. If fixed costs are small relative to the size of the market, as was the case for many pioneer Internet companies, then firms with no more than, say, 5 percent of the market are still able to compete on almost equal terms with established incumbents. It is hard to keep newcomers out of these markets, and consequently the established firms suffer death from a thousand cuts, as each entrant takes a small part of the business, but the parts add up. However, if fixed costs are large relative to the size of the market—meaning that the market is small relative to the infrastructure required—the potential entrant may have to win 25 percent or more of the business in order to close the cost gap with established firms. As long as there is some level of customer loyalty, through habit, inertia, or the other features that make customers stick, it is the rare entrant that can reach this level of penetration, and economy-of-scale advantages are an effective barrier to entry.

General Motors, Ford, and Chrysler had their profitability undermined largely by the growth in the global car market. When American consumers had distinct national tastes in automobile features and designs, foreign manufacturers were faced with the enormous hurdle of winning a large share of the U.S. auto market in order to support the fixed costs of designing, producing, promoting, and distributing the cars they intended to export to the United States. But things changed starting in the 1970s, when high fuel prices made American tastes more like those of other developed countries. The result was the transformation of the U.S. market from distinctively American to global. The Japanese companies had already invested in the fixed costs necessary to design, engineer, and manufacture their low-mileage cars. With these fixed costs now spread over global sales, foreign car companies could prosper in the United

States with a smaller share of the U.S. market. They still needed the additional fixed costs of a distribution and service network to enter the U.S. market, but it was an investment they could afford. They were aided here because, by tradition and by law, the dealership networks were independent of GM, Ford, and Chrysler. Thus veteran dealers were free to establish parallel operations to carry the imported cars and could remain profitable even as the domestic manufacturers were struggling. The expansion of the global market for fuel-efficient cars substantially reduced barriers to entry and ultimately impaired the profitability of U.S. companies and of British and other nationally focused auto companies as well.

Coca-Cola has had a very different experience. In its business, the costs of distribution, advertising, and sales are a major part of the total cost structure. Because these are all incurred within local markets and need to be replicated in each region in which the companies operate, fixed costs remain large relative to the size of each of these separate markets. Thus, global growth in sales has not affected the economies of scale advantages that Coca-Cola (and Pepsi) enjoys in each of these distinct markets. An entrant has to incur the fixed costs of advertising, distribution, and sales on a market-by-market basis in order to compete, and it needs to reach an adequate scale—say 20 percent of the local market—in order to diminish the economies of scale advantage of the two big cola companies. So, whatever the growth in demand globally, each local market is difficult for an entrant to penetrate and challenge the incumbent firms. As a consequence, Coca-Cola (and Pepsi and a few other domestic companies) has not faced the challenge of a Nippon Cola or a Great Wall Cola or a Taj Mahal Lemon-Lime Soda. Quite the contrary: They have been able to expand internationally, on a market-by-market basis, because there are few local incumbents with impregnable positions and the appeal of the American colas has been powerful both in developed countries and emerging ones.

The Special Role of Economies of Scale Advantages

Competitive advantages that stem from economies of scale are more durable than those dependent on proprietary technology or customer captivity.[5] Advantages due to proprietary technology tend to be limited to particular generations of technology and fade once that changes. In high-tech industries, where change is rapid, advantages based on proprietary technology disappear quickly and repeatedly, each time a new generation of technology emerges. Unless the incumbent firm has some advantage in the race for each new generation, the barriers to entry that protect it from competition will have a limited life span. Eventually, it will face unrestrained entry and strenuous competition.

Customer captivity has similar characteristics. Existing customers may be tied to a product or service, but virgin customers—those new to a market—are up for grabs. As existing customers age, die, or move away, the advantages of customer captivity dissipate with them. Unless the incumbent firm has a leg up in acquiring new customers, the barriers to entry based on customer captivity will eventually disappear.

Advantages based on economies of scale provide incumbents with a lead in the acquisition of new technologies and new customers, allowing them to rejuvenate and strengthen advantages that may have been fading. Consider the case of Intel, which competes with Advanced Micro Devices (AMD) in the market for central processing units (CPUs) for desktop computers and servers. Intel and AMD sell these processors to computer manufacturers. These buyers have demonstrated a preference for dealing with Intel, based on Intel's reputation with consumers, a long experience of satisfaction with the quality and availability of its offerings, and the uncertainties involved with placing their entire futures in the hands of a secondary company like AMD, whose ability to supply chips on a large scale is untested. Because of customer preferences, if Intel produces the best chip of a certain generation, it can expect to capture virtually the whole market. If AMD comes up with a superior chip, which it occasionally has, it will be lucky to win a quarter of the market. Many manufacturers wait to see whether Intel can catch up in a reasonable time before they make any commitment to AMD.

Because it is so much larger, Intel can afford to spend many times as much as AMD on designing and producing new generations of chip technology. There are economies of scale in research and development, essentially a fixed cost for each chip generation, that provide Intel with lower average unit costs and more profit from each chip sold. So it goes into the competition for each successive generation able to afford a much larger budget for research and development. Though AMD does on occasion produce a better chip, Intel has the resources to catch up and surpass it in the next round. In its history, AMD has learned how difficult it is to translate a temporary victory into successive triumphs against its much-better-funded rival. And Intel has seen how economies of scale can transform temporary advantages in proprietary technology into long-lived ones.

Economies of scale advantages can also help companies that have captive customers keep them and find replacements when needed. In the soda business, bottling and distribution are done locally, even for national brands. Thanks to the economies of scale in distribution, Coca-Cola can offer its products more extensively and at lower cost to both virgin and existing customers. It has an advantage in recruiting new customers over smaller entrants with their higher costs and narrower product availability. Advertising in any particular market is a fixed cost; it does not generally change with the number of units sold. With its large and loyal base of local customers, Coke (and Pepsi) can afford to spend more on advertising both to maintain existing customers and to win new ones. Any small competitor that sought to match this advertising would have to spend much more of its revenues, an expensive and often money-losing response. So, in the race for those who have not yet made a cola commitment, the large existing companies are at a great advantage.[6] Thanks to economies of scale and the large advertising and promotion budget they permit, companies like Coca-Cola can transform short-term customer captivity into long-term market dominance. Economies of scale, properly managed, can be a self-perpetuating competitive advantage.

Competitive Advantages in a Global World

Advantages based on economies of scale are the most durable in protecting incumbent firms from the unbridled competition that eliminates profits. Profitability therefore depends on the ability of a firm to dominate a particular market. The chances are small that one or even several firms will be able to dominate large global markets, such as that for automobiles. There is simply room for too many competitors. In a global world, the way to profitability above the cost of capital is to dominate local markets. For service businesses, where goods are both produced and consumed locally, this means focusing on markets that are literally—geographically—local. For example, a company such as Oxford Health Plans, the largest health maintenance company in the New York metropolitan area, has powerful scale advantages over a competitor like Aetna, which has more clients nationally but a relatively small share of the New York market. Doctors want to affiliate with Oxford because it has more insured clients; clients are attracted because it has more doctors, including those they may already be using. All of Aetna's clients and doctors in Chicago, Dallas, or Los Angeles are irrelevant because they have no bearing on the service area. In addition to these network advantages, Oxford benefits from economies of scale advantages by being able to spread its local fixed administrative costs over a larger local customer base. As long as it focuses on the New York region, Oxford will be more profitable than Aetna. However, if Aetna dominates any of its geographic markets, it will be in the same position as Oxford for that locality.

The same structure applies to the retail industries. Supermarket chains are most profitable where they dominate local markets (Figure 4.1). In this industry, local fixed costs include advertising, distribution, and local store management. For a chain with a dense concentration of stores in a local

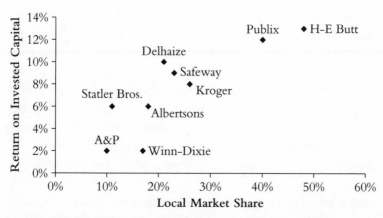

Figure 4.1   Supermarket Profitability and Market Share
Source: Accenture, Grocery Study High Performance Characteristics, September 2003.

market, capable managers can supervise a large number of units without having to spend much time traveling. Management supervision is crucial in an industry that employs many lower-paid and short-term workers. The difference between a well-run and a poorly managed store, obvious to customers who usually have a choice among supermarkets, is a key factor in company profitability.

The history of the world's largest retailer, Wal-Mart, demonstrates the importance of local dominance to a company's profitability. Sam Walton's original strategy was to be the leading—and often the only—discount retailer in his Arkansas region. When Wal-Mart expanded, it did so from the center outward, allowing it to use its existing distribution and management infrastructure in the adjacent markets into which it was moving. Compared to Kmart, Wal-Mart's disciplined approach made it much more profitable than its more geo-graphically diffuse rival, which ultimately went into bank-ruptcy. But Wal-Mart lost that edge when it decided to expand internationally. It entered markets where there were power-ful established competitors that enjoyed the same competi-tive advantages in their backyards that had allowed Wal-Mart to prosper in its U.S. regions. As we have seen, Wal-Mart ulti-mately had the sense to withdraw from both South Korea and Germany. It has had better results in Canada and Mexico, con-tiguous to its U.S. stronghold.

Markets can also be local in the figurative sense of a product space, and companies that operate in these local prod-uct markets can also benefit from barriers to entry and earn superior returns, even in a global world. The history of the personal computer industry illustrates the advantages of domi-nating a local product market. IBM and Apple, two companies that tried to encompass the whole industry in their early years, had much less success than Intel and Microsoft, which focused on narrow product segments. Intel secured its position when, unlike many of its competitors, it abandoned the market for memory chips and focused on the CPU. Its profitability soared, and it has maintained its leading share in this market. Microsoft began by dominating the operating systems for personal computers. As that business grew, it expanded into adjacent software markets, especially office applications, where it could take advantage of its position in operating systems. This disciplined strategy, which paralleled Wal-Mart's approach of expanding from an established core into adjacent territories, made Microsoft ridiculously profitable and, for a brief while at least, the largest company by market capitalization in the world. But in recent years, it has diversified into videogames, network services, portable music players, and other industries remote from its core business. Not surprisingly, none of these have come close to matching the successes it has had in operating systems or office applications.

One of the great paradoxes of globalization is that as markets have become more global, the successful companies have been those, such as the leading Chinese firms, that are locally focused. They have been able to dominate their local markets, local in either the geographic or the product-space sense, where competitive advantages can be created and sustained. They have also resisted the siren's call to expand abroad into markets where other firms are already entrenched. Through wisdom or luck, the successful firms have avoided the big global markets such as automobiles, consumer electronics, and other manufactures that can no longer be dominated by a small handful of companies. The companies that have been able to compete successfully across national boundaries, such as News Corp in media and HSBC in finance, increasingly see themselves not as global companies but as multilocal ones, native in each of the many markets in which they operate.

Table 4.1   McDonald's Profitability

Period	Return on Sales 2004–2006	Return on Assets 2006
United States	34.7%	26.9%
Europe	21.1%	15.0%
Canada	18.1%	14.5%
Asia, Pacific, Middle East	10.6%	8.1%
Latin America	1.6%	1.5%

SOURCE: McDonald's annual reports.

Even companies with great international brand names, like McDonald's, have not been able to overcome the disadvantages of playing far from home. Nowhere does McDonald's profitability abroad equal its success in the United States. In Europe and Canada, the territories most densely populated by the Golden Arches, its performance has been much better than in Asia or Latin America. Local dominance matters, even for a product—the Big Mac—so ubiquitous that it is used by *The Economist* to compare the purchasing power of dozens of national currencies. (See Table 4.1.)

The Future of Profitability

Where globalization creates large, global markets, such as those for automobiles, memory chips, appliances, and other manufacturers, in place of smaller, national ones, it has been and will continue to be the scourge of profitability. Companies that once enjoyed economies-of-scale advantages within their home markets will have to learn to live without that barrier to

entry. There is, however, a powerful countertrend that accounts
for the recent increases in profitability among the economies
of the United States, Europe, and Japan. Markets for services are inherently more local than markets for manufacturers. They are more easily protected by barriers to entry based
on local economies of scale. Profitability in the service sector
is also inherently higher than manufacturing profitability and
less vulnerable to the effects of globalization. One study by the
Bank of England calculated that for the United States and the
United Kingdom—the countries with the largest and most
efficient service sectors—average returns on capital in services
from 1990 to 2001 were 18.1 percent and 13.6 percent respectively. Comparable returns on capital in the overall economies
were 8.1 percent and 11.5 percent. And there is no evidence
that returns on services have been declining since 2000, in the
era of Globalization 3.0. Because the service sector is growing
as a share of national income, higher profitability here should
more than offset the decline in profitability in the manufacturing sector, which globalization may continue to undermine.

Even in manufacturing, there may be some favorable trends
that run counter to the overall movement. Companies such as
John Deere in agricultural equipment and Hoffman LaRoche
in pharmaceuticals are finding that as pure manufacturing costs
decline, due to increases in productivity, marketing, service support, and distribution make up a larger share of overall operations within the firm. These are locally based activities and can
be protected by the same local economies-of-scale advantages
that protect more obviously service businesses, such as telecommunications. The returns on these activities may ultimately
offset the negative effects of global competition even in more
purely manufacturing industries.

Businesses that focus on dominating local—in both
senses—markets have little to fear from globalization and much

to gain from the trend toward services. Also, the damage to the profitability of pure manufacturing companies in the developed world has already happened. It is an old and familiar tale, and while we may mourn the passing of General Motors and the prosperity it brought to hundreds of thousands of factory workers, we are not likely to see the story repeat itself in the service economy of the future.[7]

Chapter 5

International Finance in a Global World

Home Field Advantage

In early 1997, Kwan Ju was happily established as a middle manager for a major South Korean Bank. His standard of living was unprecedented by historical South Korean measures, and he had little anxiety about the future. The South Korean economy had been growing rapidly for over 40 years with only a few bumps along the way, and it was continuing to thrive despite a nagging deficit in its external balance of payments that it financed largely with debt from abroad. The principal topic of public discussion was a potential rapprochement with North Korea.

On May 14 and 15, Thailand's currency, the *baht*, was sold off by speculators and dropped significantly. In June, the central bank of Thailand announced that there would be no devaluation. That policy lasted until July 2, when Thailand was forced to devalue the baht by from 12 to 15 percent. By August, with its economy melting down and the finance minister resigning, Thailand had been forced to go cap in hand to the International Monetary Fund for a $16 billion rescue package. It presented an austerity budget required by the IMF that sharply reduced government spending. But so far, these problems in Thailand seemed too distant from Kwan Ju's life in South Korea to cause any concern.

Still, the Malaysian *ringgit* had also come under attack and declined sharply, as had the Indonesian *rupiah*. In July, Malaysia ceased to support its currency and, like Thailand, began to suffer a severe economic contraction. Local firms could not pay the interest on loans denominated in dollars or yen, and many of them started to fail. On August 14, Indonesia announced that it would no longer support the rupiah, and its value promptly collapsed. This drop was followed by the now-familiar pattern of failing companies, economic contraction, and pursuit of an IMF bailout ($40 billion in this case) along with the requisite austerity budget plan. Despite all this turmoil in his neighborhood, Kwan Ju was not yet worried, comforted by the knowledge that South Korea was much more developed than Thailand, Malaysia, or Indonesia.

It took only a few months for that confidence to confront the reality of a sinking currency. The South Korean *won* had maintained its value of between 890 and 900 to the dollar throughout the summer, but in September it fell to 913 won per dollar (more won to the dollar means lower value of the won) on the way to 953 won to dollar on October 28. At the start of November, the finance minister insisted that the won would never be allowed to fall below 1,000 to the dollar and that South Korea would not require an IMF bailout package, with all the pain that that entailed. Sixteen days later, the authorities capitulated and announced they could no longer support the won; the exchange rate was then 1,009 to the dollar. On November 21, they sought help from the IMF. By the middle of February 1998, the won was trading at 1,700 per dollar, a decline of almost 50 percent since the previous summer. South Korean firms and banks, unable to service their dollar- or yen-denominated debt (estimated to account for $120 billion out of a total debt of $360 billion), were failing in large numbers. Even banks with available resources stopped lending money, and the ensuing credit crunch made things worse. Unable to finance production and investment, firms began to shrink their operations and lay off workers. Between September 1997 and February 1998, the South Korean stock market index declined from over 800 to below 280, a drop of more than 65 percent.

Kwan Ju, with much of his savings having evaporated, was laid off in March 1998. His experience was shared by millions of people in developing or recently developed economies, and it was widely attributed to globalization.

Flow of Funds

Financial markets are the one area where globalization appears to have had an unambiguous impact. The critical symptoms that first appeared in the mid-to-late 1980s have now become almost numbingly familiar. A developing economy implements financial markets and other reforms with the hope of attracting foreign capital to stimulate growth. The policy succeeds. Growth generates demands for imported goods, both equipment for firms and consumer goods for households. In China and some other countries, exports more than pay for this demand for imports. But elsewhere, export earnings are not large enough to cover the costs, and these countries need to borrow from abroad to fill the gap.[1]

At first, foreign lenders are eager to accommodate this demand for funds. However, because they are unwilling to take on the additional risk of having the loans repaid in the local currency, which may depreciate, the debts are denominated in an international currency such as dollars. At the same time, foreign investors may help out by purchasing securities issued by governments, banks, and businesses in the now growing local economy. Over time, as the developing country continues to import more than it exports, foreigners come to hold more of its debt and its securities. The basic imbalance is exacerbated by interest and dividend payments, which grow along with the size of the debt and the number of shares owned abroad. At some point, there is a day of reckoning, and it is not pretty.

The denouement looks something like this: Foreign investors become nervous and begin to sell their holdings. They get paid in the local currency, which they do not want to hold. So they exchange (sell) won for dollars or some other stable currency. These transactions drive down the value of the won. An initial decline, say from $.0011 to $.0010 per won, leads other foreign investors to sell their holdings, which are now worth less in dollars. The local citizenry, with local assets to sell, also try to unload whatever they can and move the proceeds into safer currencies abroad, into accounts they have previously established or scramble to open. Panic builds, and everyone seeks to sell won and won-denominated assets before the value of the won sinks even further. The won may drop quickly to half or even less of its former exchange rate. The prices of local stocks and other assets, even though they are measured in won, also drop because people are liquidating them as quickly as they can to obtain won, which can be sold for stronger foreign currencies. The downward spiral is relentless.

The nominal wealth of local households falls with the decline in price of these local securities. The financial positions of local firms, such as banks, that own won assets also worsen. At the same time, there is a massive increase in the burden of servicing the previously incurred debt denominated in foreign currencies. Interest payments, measured in the local currency, have increased as the exchange value of that currency has fallen. Interest payments of $10 million at 1,000 won to the dollar could have been covered by an income of 10 billion won. But with the won at 2,000 per dollar, it takes an income of 20 billion won. Local firms and households stagger under the burden and must curtail spending, hiring, and output. Banks, whose balance sheets have deteriorated, try to call in the now-risky loans and stop making new ones. The resulting credit drought causes further reductions in spending, hiring, and output. There are widespread layoffs, the demand for goods collapses, and an economic contraction of Depression-era proportions follows.

This sequence of events occurred first in Mexico in 1986. It reappeared with special virulence in Asia in 1997, when South Korea, Thailand, Indonesia, and Malaysia all suffered major economic crises. In 1998 and 1999, Mexico, Russia, and Brazil were afflicted. In each case, an initial short and sharp collapse was followed by a long, painful recovery. The first major antiglobalization demonstrations emerged at a World Trade Organization summit meeting in Seattle in late fall 1999, in the wake of these experiences.

Notwithstanding these dramatic episodes, the overall impact of globalization in financial markets, as elsewhere, has been exaggerated. The turbulence of the late 1990s (and into 2001 if Argentina is included) has subsided. The East Asian countries seem to have succeeded in immunizing themselves against a recurrence by running sustained balance-of-payment surpluses. Like China and India, they have limited their reliance on foreign financing. Russia has benefited from high oil and other natural resource prices, removing the need and the temptation to rely on overseas sources of funds. While there is no guarantee that the pattern of events that beset South Korea and the other countries in the late 1990s will not recur (see Chapter 6), the ability of individual countries to protect themselves by forgoing extensive foreign financing should limit their frequency and magnitude.

However, the capacity of countries with inadequate local savings to rely on external sources of foreign capital has been widely claimed as one of the major benefits of financial market globalization. Yet here again the impact of globalization has been exaggerated. Inflows of foreign capital can take two forms. In one, generally called *portfolio investment*, foreigners invest financially in a country by either making loans or buying publicly traded financial assets, including stocks, government debt, corporate bonds, local bank certificates of deposit, and other instruments. In the other form, called *direct investment*, foreigners invest by building factories, installing capital equipment, or otherwise developing local business enterprises. In fact, neither portfolio investment nor foreign direct investment (FDI) has been a major source of long-term financing for capital-poor or developing countries.

Foreign Direct Investment: Not Where the Action Is

We might not expect FDI to be a significant source of capital for developed countries like the United States. As the figures in Table 5.1 indicate, the foreign share of total fixed investment in the United States, in things such as housing, equipment, and other physical structures, is small and has been declining since 2000. What may surprise us is that the BRIC countries (Brazil, Russia, India, China), the largest and most robust of the newly emergent economies, look very much like the United States in the proportion of their fixed asset investments coming from

Table 5.1   Foreign Direct Investment Level (Percent of Gross Fixed Investment)

Country	Average 2000–2006	2000	2001	2002	2003	2004	2005	2006
United States	7.1	16.2	8.5	4.4	3.2	6.0	4.5	7.1
Brazil	17.6	11.9	10.4	10.8	8.9	8.6	6.9	NA
Russia	8.4							
India	4.0							
China	8.5							
U.K.	28.6	31.0	13.9	12.1	8.7	8.6	20.4	16.3
Germany	13.4							
France	16.0							
Italy	5.6							
Japan	0.5	3.3	1.6	1.3	1.3	2.7	1.5	0.4
South Korea	2.9							
Canada	17.5	35.1	20.9	15.4	8.4	8.4	15.0	18.2
Mexico	15.0							

foreign sources. The small total—6.9 percent in 2005, the last year for which figures are available—has been trending down since 2000.

With the exception of Brazil, FDI did not average as much as 10 percent of the total during this period. If these countries are to become the new giants of the global economy, they will do so without significant FDI. For other developing countries, especially the very poor ones largely in Africa, FDI is equally insignificant.

There is more cross-border direct investment within regions such as the European Union or North America. France and Germany received FDI equal to about 15 percent of the total between 2000 and 2006. The United Kingdom, with an average of almost 30 percent, was by far the largest recipient.

However, in the EU, as in the United States and the BRIC countries, the trend was either level or down between 2000 and 2006. The economies of Mexico and Canada, closely tied to the United States, had average FDI levels of 15 and 17 percent, respectively, over the period from 2000 to 2006. In both countries, the trend was down, with the partial exception of energy investments in Canada after 2004.

Japan and South Korea after the crisis of 1997 hardly received any FDI at all. FDI averaged 3.3 percent in the two countries in 2000. By 2006, it had shrunk almost to the vanishing point.

If FDI is an important indicator of the globalization of capital markets, then there is not much to it. FDI accounts on average for just about 10 percent of capital formation in the period between 2000 and 2006 and there is less of it at the end than at the beginning.

Financial Markets and Portfolio Investment: Not Here, Either

That still leaves open the possibility that global integration might be occurring within financial markets for trading securities. Portfolio investments, rather than investment in real assets, might be the way in which capital is redeployed from rich countries to poor ones. The benefits of this global investment might outweigh the associated risks of financial instability. In fact, the history of financial markets indicates that this has not happened. And the underlying nature of financial markets makes it unlikely ever to take place.

In a market economy, financial markets serve two basic functions. First, they provide liquidity, a means for owners to convert their current holdings into cash if and when they need or want to. This ability is an important inducement to investment. If entrepreneurs and venture capitalists could not, at some point, sell their shares of an operating business for ready cash, whether for consumption, diversification, or some other purpose, they might be less likely to take the initial risky steps of creating and expanding the enterprise. Also, people who buy shares during their working years, when they are accumulating assets, will want to sell them and consume the proceeds when they retire. Thanks to their liquidity, financial markets for publicly traded securities are an efficient way to transfer assets among wealth owners. Because of the ease they provide in turning securities into cash, financial markets also serve as an inducement to savings in the first place.

Second, financial markets transfer funds from wealth-owning savers to operating businesses, which then invest the money in factories, equipment, research and development, and other assets essential to their operations and growth. This transfer does not take place when existing securities are traded; trading just moves securities from one portfolio to another, without any capital going to the companies that can invest it. Only when new securities—shares, bonds, notes, and some more exotic instruments—are sold to investors by companies and financial institutions do savings get transformed into productive assets. For economic development, this is the function of financial markets that matters.

A look at the record reveals that it hasn't mattered much. Savings rates may be high even where large and well-functioning financial markets are absent. Currently, the Chinese are saving close to half of their income with only limited access to public financial markets. These markets are a rather recent innovation, yet savings rates around the world have been high since 1900. Because economic development relies on channeling those savings into business investment, we need to ask how this movement has happened.

Institutions as Investors:
These Do Matter

There are two basic channels for converting savings into business investment. One is the sale of securities in public financial markets, which is the most commonly discussed if only because the markets themselves get so much attention. The other channel is institutional. Banks, insurance companies, credit unions, venture capital firms, and corporations themselves raise funds in their normal course of business, without necessarily selling securities in public markets. Banks accept deposits, insurance companies collect premiums, and corporations generate earnings that they can reinvest in their operations. Venture capital firms gather subscriptions from investors, both individuals and institutions such as pension funds, endowments, and insurance companies. Though some of these funds may be used to purchase publicly traded securities, helping to keep that market liquid, they are also invested directly in the businesses, as loans or equity shares, as part of the ongoing relationship between the institution and the businesses it supports.

This continuing relationship is what distinguishes institutional investments from public market sources of funds. In a public market, the securities can change hands every day—many times within the day, in extreme cases—and ownership is likely to be widely dispersed among many investors, who want to diversify their own risks and so hold baskets of securities. These public market investors cannot, despite their best efforts, follow in detail all the actions and evolutions of the firms on which they hold claims. Institutional investors, on the other hand, are able to monitor their investments continuously. They have extensive information about what is happening inside the business, and they have long-term relationships with the executives. They are much less likely to be surprised by a press release or a periodic earnings report.

Good information and careful monitoring are at the heart of successful investing, so it is not surprising that institutions, which have the information and do the monitoring, are a far more important source of funds for operating businesses than are public securities markets.

Investors, whether institutional or public market, have two fundamental concerns. First, there is the question of what the operators of the business will do with the funds entrusted to them. Ideally, the managers should be governed by an incentive structure that aligns their interest perfectly with the interests of the investors. But in practice, a perfect alignment is impossible. One reason is that owners of the equity do not have interests identical to owners of the debt. Lenders get no extra reward if the firm does exceptionally well, so they are reluctant to endorse some risks that stock owners, who do benefit from increases in earnings, may favor. Managers inevitably have interests of their own, such as building an empire or doing adventurous things like cutting-edge research and development, that may not pay off for investors. No formal reward structure can fully offset these desires. Finally, as the controller of information about business performance, management can manipulate that information to serve its own ends.

This misalignment of interests between managers and investors introduces the problem of *moral hazard* into the process by which the funds within the firm are put to use. The people making the decisions (managers) have a different attitude toward risk than the investors whose money is at stake. Managers are more likely to expose the company to more risk, because the payoff is greater for them and the losses smaller. Once the funds are within the firm, it is the managers who decide how they are used. Institutional investors, which have the ability and the incentive to monitor closely what is going on, are much better positioned to protect their interests than distant and diversified owners of publicly traded securities. They are better able to limit the moral hazard problem.

The second issue that concerns investors is the terms on which the funds are provided. For example, when the management of a publicly traded company decides to issue new shares, the shares are priced at or near the existing market price. That price represents what investors, on average, think about the company's future prospects, a judgment based on publicly available information. Management, on the other hand, has more accurate and detailed private information about what the company's real prospects are. It sees whether new products are moving successfully through the development pipeline, it sees costs trends on items it buys and sells and it sees its current order book and has a sense of how major customers are reacting to the new and existing products and services it sells. Management, in other words, sees all the cards in play, not merely the ones that have been exposed. Armed with this knowledge, how likely is it that management will sell new shares if it thinks the current market price underestimates the company's future prospects? Conversely, if management's private information indicates that the company is overvalued by the market, it has every reason to sell as many shares as it can, collect the cash, and fortify the balance sheet.

This imbalance in information between insiders (management) and outsiders (the market) means that new issues of stock will tend to be offered by companies whose shares are overpriced. Bond issues share a similar imbalance.[2] Companies are more likely to issue bonds when they think the interest rates they have to pay underestimate the risks involved.

Investors in both equity and debt are aware of this situation, which makes them suspicious of new issues, especially equity, by existing companies. The information imbalance creates the problem of *adverse selection*. Groucho Marx's oft-quoted line, that he would never join a club that would have him as a member, is an illustration of adverse selection. Since the club knew its membership standards better than the applicant, the fact that Groucho exceeded those standards meant that it wasn't the club for him.

From an investor's viewpoint, the adverse selection problem has the same solution as the moral hazard problem, which is continuing access to inside information about a company's present condition and its likely performance in the future. Institutions are much better positioned to handle this function, including accepting limitations on their use and disclosure of private information, than is a dispersed and anonymous body of public investors.

The historical record supports the argument that institutional mechanisms are preferred over public markets for deploying funds from savers to operating businesses. The figures in Table 5.2 come from a study done in the latter 1980s of the sources of company finance in large industrial economies between 1980 and 1985. These economies had the most developed public financial markets, yet in all of them, retained earnings and institutional debt accounted for 90 percent or more of company capital. The minimal portion accounted for by market financing actually overstates its importance, since in countries such as Japan, Italy, and Germany, a large portion of those securities were permanently placed within financial institutions such as banks and insurance companies.

Despite its age, the study is still relevant. The state of development of public financial markets in countries such as France, Germany, and Italy was similar then to the current situation in developing economies like China, India, Brazil, and Russia. But even in the large, developed economies, things have not

Table 5.2   Net Financing of Nonfinancial Enterprises, 1980–1985
(Percent of Total Financing)

Country	Canada	France	Germany	Italy	Japan	U.K.	United States
Retained Earnings	74.5%	57.6%	75.8%	58.1%	50.3%	97.0%	69.8%
Institutional Debt	14.8%	35.0%	24.6%	31.0%	43.8%	7.2%	19.8%
Public Debt	8.3%	1.5%	−1.1%	1.8%	1.8%	−1.0%	9.4%
Public Equity	2.4%	5.9%	0.6%	9.2%	4.0%	−3.1%	0.9%

SOURCE: Colin Mayer, "Financial Systems, Corporate Finance, and Economic Development," in Glenn Hubbard, ed., *A Symmetric Information, Corporate Finance, and Investment*. Chicago, University of Chicago Press, 1990.

changed much in the interim. In Table 5.3, the sources of financing for Microsoft, Intel, and Wal-Mart are presented for the years 1994 and 2006. These are the three largest companies to have come to prominence in the last 15 years. Only Intel relied on significant external financing, and even here it amounted to 10 percent of equity in 1994. After 1994, none of these companies raised any money by selling equity in public markets. Microsoft and Intel actually bought back large quantities of stock. Wal-Mart, the one company of the three to rely on much debt, was financed largely by institutional debt in its early years, and only later did it sell bonds in the public market.

The balance sheets of established companies outside the United States, such as the Japanese automobile and motorcycle company Honda and the Swiss pharmaceutical giant Roche Group, parent of Hoffman-LaRoche, look similar to those of the American firms (Table 5.4). Public financial markets are not a significant source of capital even for these global giants, which have the best access to them. The important sources are either

Table 5.3 Incremental and Total Financing, 1994 and 2006 ($ billions)

	Wal-Mart			Intel			Microsoft		
	1994	2006	Change	1994	2006	Change	1994	2006	Change
Sales	82.5	345.0	262.5	16.2	35.4	19.2	4.7	51.2	46.6
Assets	32.8	151.2	118.4	17.5	48.4	30.9	5.4	63.2	57.8
Cash	0.0	7.4	7.3	2.5	6.6	4.1	3.6	23.4	19.8
Debt	11.6	35.2	23.6	0.7	2.0	1.3	0	0	0
Net debt	*11.5*	*27.8*	*16.3*	*(1.7)*	*(4.6)*	*(2.9)*	*(3.6)*	*(23.4)*	*(19.8)*
Equity	12.7	61.6	48.9	12.1	36.8	24.6	4.5	31.1	26.6
Retained Earnings	12.0	58.3	46.4	9.6	28.9	19.4	3.0	n/a	n/a
External	0.2	0.2	0	1.2	1.2	0	0	0	0
ESOPs, Acquisitions, etc.	0.6	3.1	2.5	1.4	6.6	5.2	1.5	n/a	n/a

SOURCE: Company financial statements.

Table 5.4   Incremental and Total Financing, 2004 and 2006

	Honda (B Yen)			Roche Group (MSF)		
	2002	2006	Change	2002	2006	Change
Sales	7,632	9,908	2,276	29,725	42,041	12,316
Assets	6,786	12,037	5,251	63,211	74,414	11,203
Cash	609	946	337	15,825	24,331	8,506
Net debt	*1,551*	*2,981*	*1,430*	*6,525*	*(16,088)*	*(22,613)*
Equity	2,610	4,483	1,873	20,810	46,814	26,004
Paid In	258	258	0	160	160	0
Retained	2,766	4,694	1,928	26,503	39,284	12,781
Other*	(414)	(469)	(55)	(5,853)	7,370**	n/a

* Predominantly share repurchases.
** Minority interest.
Source: Company financial statements.

retained earnings or loans from financial institutions. Venture capital, another institutional source, played an important role during the startup phases.

Safer at Home: Financial Markets and the Limits of Globalization

Public financial markets serve the function of providing liquidity by allowing investors to trade securities efficiently and openly. But the far more important function of deploying capital from savers to business investment is carried out predominantly by institutions, not markets. These funds are entrusted to the institutions because of their ability to collect information on and monitor the performance of the enterprises they bankroll. The enterprises operate locally; South Korean firms are run from South Korea, even when they have major exports and branches overseas. An awareness of global trends in automobile markets may be useful for banks or insurance companies lending to a South Korean automaker, but it is less important than knowing how the company is doing in cost reduction, product development, labor relations, quality control, working capital management, and capital spending. It also helps to have continuing and candid relationships with the company's management. Locally based institutions, with large and permanent stakes in these firms, are much better situated than impersonal and global financial markets to keep track of what is going on and to intervene when things go off course.

Also, though global companies may get the lion's share of headlines, most business is entirely local. As services gain a larger share of economic activity, the dominance of the local will only increase. Housing, for example, is a local industry, and the capital that housing requires, whether as construction loans for developers or mortgages for homebuyers, is best provided by local institutions that have knowledge of the real estate markets, construction trends, and the creditworthiness of the borrower. When this financing is ultimately provided by distant and ignorant investors—and no financial instruments have yet been devised that are more effective than mortgage-backed bonds at shaking money out of distant and ignorant investors—then all the protection provided by local knowledge is forsaken, to the grief of anyone left holding the debt. Banking services, including account management, consumer loans, and credit card activity, are mostly local. So, local banks, in which clients have accounts and with which they have had longstanding relationships, are likely to be much better at judging the creditworthiness of local borrowers than recently established branches of foreign banks.

Given the importance of detailed local information in capital deployment, we should expect that local institutions will be the most important sources of financing on their home turf. South Korean banks will dominate banking in Korea, German insurance companies will dominate insurance markets in Germany, and venture capital firms in the United States will lead venture capital investing in the United States.[3] In fact, that is exactly what happens. Banks such as Lloyds, Barclays, and National Westminster are identifiably British, and they dominate banking in Britain. American banks such as Citibank, JPMorgan Chase, Bank of America, Wells Fargo, and Wachovia dominate banking in the United States. Chinese banks dominate China, and so on. Only a few banks, like HSBC, have truly global ambitions. The same conditions apply in insurance and mortgage lending.

Global expansion by financial institutions has been markedly unsuccessful (Table 5.5). Even HSBC, which is among the best global financial operations, has been far more profitable in its core Asian markets than elsewhere. Though it bills itself as the "local" global bank, its profitability declines uniformly

Table 5.5　International Banking Performance, 2004–2006 Return on Assets

Bank	Home Market	Asia	Europe	North America
HSBC	2.00% (Hong Kong)	1.85%	0.94%	1.21%
Deutschebank	0.78% (Germany)	—	0.53%	0.51%
Barclay's	3.09% (U.K.)	—	1.19%	1.80%

NOTE: The underlying pattern is clear. When foreign institutions such as Deutsche Bank attempt to enter overseas mortgage loan markets, as in the United States, the evidence supports the theory that they will be operating at a significant informational disadvantage to local competitors. No one should have been surprised when they reported large losses from these initiatives.

SOURCE: Company financial statements and filings.

with declining local market presence. Table 5.5 presents similar data for other large, would-be global banks. Global U.S banks, such as Citicorp and JPMorgan Chase, perform similarly but report their international performance less uniformly. Citicorp breaks out overseas and U.S. return on capital for some businesses, such as consumer banking. From 2000 on, returns in the United States averaged about 23 percent, and overseas returns 16 percent.⁻⁺

In the essential role of channeling funds from the people who save to the businesses that invest, financial institutions, not public securities markets, are central to the process, and these institutions are far more effective locally than globally.

Global Capital Markets and Economic Development: More Headlines Than Production Lines

The public financial markets that are global do perform a role in moving funds from savers to investors, but it is a relatively minor one and it comes with significant costs. If the total volume of local savings is inadequate to support the capital investments necessary for economic development, then flows of capital from foreign sources may fill the gap. That is the theory—that capital, in search of higher returns, will flow to places where the demand for it is unmet. In practice, this flow happens less frequently than the theory suggests, and for some obvious reasons. First, as we discussed in Chapter 2, the primary engine of economic growth and development is the steady gains in efficiency within local business operations. These improvements may require some capital investments, but because they produce such high returns on the money invested, there is generally no shortage of funding. Second, as economies begin to grow rapidly, people tend to adapt only slowly to the fact that their higher incomes are sustainable. As a result, household consumption generally lags behind household income, and the savings rate rises sharply. Europe after World War II, the United States, Japan and other Asian countries, and most visibly, China today have all followed this pattern. Local savings are usually sufficient to meet local investment needs.

Historically, national savings rates have been highly correlated with national investment rates (measured as capital formation as a fraction of GDP), which would not have occurred if global financial markets were moving large amounts of savings across national boundaries. When imbalances have occurred between local savings and investment needs, they have often looked like the situation in China today. The Chinese are saving more than they can invest at home, and China is a major exporter of financial capital, as was Japan before it. Instead of money moving into developing economies, it is moving out from them to businesses and governments in the developed countries.

There are a number of instances in which savers in rich countries have invested in developing countries. South Korea, Thailand, Indonesia, Malaysia, Russia, Brazil, and Argentina have all raised funds overseas, especially for public infrastructure and development projects. When countries have poorly functioning tax systems, borrowings from abroad may be the only available source of funding for key ventures. But the inescapable fact is that in many cases, countries that have not been able to collect taxes to support their own projects have governments that are ineffective in other ways. The money raised overseas has largely been wasted; sometimes it has merely offset the outflow of local private funds that were seeking safer investment havens overseas.

Large-scale and chronic borrowing from abroad exposes countries to sudden crises such as that which cost Kwan Ju his job and his savings. The damage from these crises may outweigh the benefits of net incremental financial flows into the country. If so, then controls on foreign capital movements may be beneficial to economic growth and development, contrary to economic orthodoxy. Controls may protect against the kind of predicament a number of countries in Asia experienced in the late 1990s. Also, by making it more difficult for domestic savings to be invested abroad, controls may contribute to the development of effective financial institutions. Controls on capital flows have actually been an important part of successful development strategies in Europe, in Japan, in other Asian countries like Singapore, and in China today.

Even within a single country, at least one as large as the United States, the importance of local financial institutions for economic development shows up in the data. States that made up the core of the Confederacy have had lower per-capita incomes than the national average since the Civil War, and before. Since 1950, that gap has been closing. In the period between 1950 and 1970, these six states saw the gap shrink by 14 percentage points, from 65 percent to 79 percent (Table 5.6). It fell in all of them, and the relative improvement was most pronounced in the poor states of South Carolina, Alabama, and Mississippi. In the following 20 years, the gap continued to close, but at a much smaller rate, from 79 percent of national per-capita income to 85 percent. In this second period, it was the richer states of Virginia and Georgia that did best, with Mississippi, the poorest of the poor, hardly improving at all.

No single source explains the deteriorating pace of economic catch-up. But one important contributor may have been the elimination of barriers to national banking that took

Table 5.6   Regional Development in Six Southern United States, 1950–1990

| | Income as Percent of National Average | | | Change | |
State	1950	1970	1990	1950–1970	1970–1990
Virginia	82.1%	92.6%	104.5%	10.5%	11.9%
Georgia	69.1%	84.1%	90.8%	15.0%	6.7%
North Carolina	69.1%	81.6%	86.9%	12.5%	5.3%
South Carolina	59.7%	75.1%	80.5%	15.4%	5.4%
Alabama	58.8%	73.9%	79.4%	15.1%	5.5%
Mississippi	50.5%	65.8%	66.3%	15.3%	0.5%
Average	*64.9%*	*78.9%*	*84.7%*	*14.0%*	*5.9%*

SOURCE: *Historical Statistics of the United States, Statistical Abstract of the United States.*

place after 1970. Truly national or superregional banks opened branches in these states, and the deposits they took there were more likely to be reinvested elsewhere than in local economic activities. Or, conversely, successful banks in these states, such as North Carolina National Bank, used their strong local position to acquire banks in other states and gave up their local focus. Though still headquartered in Charlotte, North Carolina, NCNB is now known as Bank of America, and it has taken over both the original Bank of America, which was based in and oriented toward California, and the former giants from New England, Fleet Bank and Bank of Boston. It seems clear that capital market liberalization, in the form of national banking, has not contributed to the pace of economic development in these Southern states, especially the poorer ones. The implication is that financial market controls seem to be at least a defensible policy and probably a beneficial one for economic development, over and above the issues of providing stability and avoiding recurrent crises.

Thanks to the ever-inventive mutual fund industry in the United States, it is now easy and probably smart for the average investor to own securities of firms and governments in other countries. But for the crucial purpose of capital deployment, financial markets are far less globally integrated than the public market activity suggests. Actual capital deployment remains largely and properly a local activity. As a result, policy prescriptions that favor capital market openness almost as a matter of creed, without regard to specific circumstances, are likely to produce limited benefits. Structural imbalances in the global financial system may render these prescriptions actually harmful because the rapid flow of funds into and out of vulnerable economies can amplify booms and busts and spread from one economy to another. The prosperity of Kwan Ju was temporarily undermined by this contagion. We turn in the next chapter to look at alternatives to the current arrangement that might support economic development while containing some of the damage that these crises can inflict.

Chapter 6

A Genuine Global Economic Problem

Replacing the Consumer of Last Resort

As John Maynard Keynes prepared for the 1944 conference at Bretton Woods, which would establish the structure of the international financial system after World War II, he had one overriding goal. He wanted to relieve Britain of the burden of having the pound sterling serve as the world's primary reserve currency by getting the U.S. dollar to assume that role in a reformed international currency system. In this effort, as in so much else, Keynes succeeded. The system, built around the newly established International Monetary Fund (IMF), has maintained the dollar as the world's currency for international transactions for more than 60 years.

Currently, the system looks like it is starting to fray, and the problems for Britain that Keynes identified prior to Bretton Woods have returned to haunt both the United States and the rest of the world economy. And just as the failures of the sterling system played, in Keynes's thinking, a significant role in the global depression of the 1930s, similar shortcomings of the current system threaten to undermine the economic performance of the United States and the rest of the world today. This is one area, today as in the past, where global economic forces are in fact a major challenge.

The Link between Reserve Currencies and Global Financial Stability

Trade between countries with different currencies has historically taken place at fixed exchange rates. For more than a century, five U.S. dollars bought about one British pound. This fixed exchange rate was originally maintained by the gold standard. The United States backed its currency with gold at around $35 per ounce. The British did the same for the pound, at £7 per ounce. The prices were built into the gold coins each country minted and into promises to redeem paper currency for gold on demand. This ability to exchange currency for gold at a fixed rate kept the dollar and the pound in a stable relation to each other. Any serious deviation would be brought back into line by arbitrageurs buying the cheaper currency, exchanging it for gold, transporting the gold to the other country, and converting it into the more expensive currency. Variation from the fixed—gold-based—exchange rate could not exceed the cost of actually doing the arbitrage transaction. So, establishing the values of national currencies in gold effectively fixed the cross-rates of exchange at which these national currencies could trade.

The problem with the gold standard was that the global supplies of gold failed to keep pace with the growth of global economic activity, and thus restricted the amount of currency a country could issue. Since currency was required for everyday economic transactions, growing economies needed more currency to accommodate an increasing level of transactions. The only alternative was for the prices at which transactions took place to decline, offsetting the growing volume of transactions. Steadily declining prices created economic problems. A world of falling prices—deflation—was a treacherous world for businesses to navigate. They generally had to pay workers and suppliers in advance of receiving payments for the goods they sold. With prices declining, they could not recover their costs. Investment in productive capacity, which expands output and employment but always carries some measure of risk, seems unattractive compared to the safe alternative of holding cash whose value—purchasing power—would appreciate steadily as prices fell. The period of the strict gold standard, not surprisingly, was a period of steadily falling prices and recurrent economic crises.

In response, countries began to adopt alternative principles in issuing currencies. Some, such as the United States, continued to maintain gold convertibility in principle, but began to issue currency in amounts that far exceeded the available supplies of gold. Some abandoned convertibility entirely but continued to maintain existing exchange rate parities. Others, such as Germany in the aftermath of World War I, issued currency without restraint and suffered from massive inflation. Countries that sought to maintain fixed exchange rates did so by intervening directly in currency markets, buying in their currency when its exchange value threatened to fall significantly below the official level, and selling when its value threatened to rise too far.

To finance these interventions, especially to halt the decline in value of the local currency, national monetary authorities had to have on hand supplies of foreign currencies or liquid assets denominated in foreign currencies. It would do no good for the Bank of France to attempt to raise the value of the franc by offering francs for francs. Instead, it would have to buy up the excess supply of francs using a currency that would be widely acceptable to sellers of francs. Prior to World War II, the most widely accepted currency for these purposes—beyond gold, of which there was an inadequate supply—was the British pound. In the language of modern international finance, sterling (the pound) was a widely held reserve currency. Other countries were generally prepared to accept sterling in exchange for their own currencies, since there was broad confidence in the strength of the British trading economy and the self-restraint of the Bank of England in issuing pounds.

As a consequence, countries tended to intervene in currency markets using pounds, and firms often carried out international transactions in pounds. As a further consequence, both public authorities and private companies had to hold stocks of liquid sterling assets to provide the reserves necessary to cover temporary imbalances between foreign inflows and outflows. In the case of the monetary authorities, these imbalances were the cause of fluctuating exchange rates. As global economies grew, and transaction volume kept pace, so did the demand for sterling reserves. Under these conditions, England had to provide a steady and steadily growing supply of liquid sterling assets to the rest of the world to keep the international financial system functioning smoothly.

Problems arose because there were only three ways for the rest of the world to increase their holdings of liquid sterling assets:

1. Borrow pounds from British financial institutions.
2. Sell real assets to the British.
3. Export more to Britain than Britain exported to the rest of the world.

The first alternative was not sustainable. If countries borrowed from Britain while running a trade deficit with it, their debts to British institutions would increase without any ultimate power of repayment. Paying interest alone required that it earn sterling on a continuing basis, and this could happen only if foreign countries sold more to Britain than they bought from it.

The second alternative posed the same problem. The returns that Britain earned on the foreign assets it had bought required payment that could be made only if the other countries exported more to Britain than they imported from it. So, in fact, the only choice for a country that needed permanent and increasing sterling reserves was to run a surplus in its current account balance—the annual difference between goods sold and bought—with Britain.

Now, if all other countries ran current account surpluses with Britain, it is axiomatic that Britain would have to run a current account deficit with the rest of the world. It has always been an inescapable fact of international economic life that every pound's worth of goods that Britain sells abroad is a pound's worth of goods bought abroad. The reverse is also obvious. Thus, if foreign sales to Britain exceed foreign purchases from Britain, then British purchases of foreign goods must exceed its sale of goods abroad. Another way of saying the same thing is that total current account surpluses and current account deficits, summed over all countries, must be zero. If the rest of the world were running current account surpluses, then Britain had to run deficits on its current account.

For Britain, there were some clear advantages in this situation. Unlike other countries, it could chronically import more from the rest of the world than it exported. Thanks to the general acceptability of pounds, Britain's current account deficit was not automatically unsustainable. Because they needed pounds for reserves, its trading partners were content to exchange them for real goods and services without much thought of ultimate repayment. Chronic current account deficits did not undermine the value of the pound, as they would have done to other, nonreserve currencies, unless and until those deficits became unmanageably large.

When the pound did decline in value relative to other currencies, the blow was softened by Britain's reserve currency status. If Austria's schilling declined in value, the burden of Austria's overseas debts—denominated in sterling—would increase dramatically. More schillings would be needed to pay the interest, and the increase in this expense might take a serious bite out of Austria's net domestic income and could even lead to widespread bankruptcy for those firms unable to meet their foreign debt obligations. For Britain, the situation was different. With its overseas debts denominated in its domestic currency, a decline in the value of the pound also reduced the amount of debt Britain owed. Those benefits were a source of envy and occasional resentment among countries without a reserve currency to call their own.

For the British, there was an offsetting and less desirable side to the pound's position as the world's reserve currency. Having foreigners sell more to Britain than Britain sold abroad meant that British domestic income was on balance directed to foreign producers. This leakage of British demand overseas created a situation in which Britain's domestic production, the source of domestic income, had a chronic tendency to exceed domestic demand. The result was a steady downward pressure on British domestic prices, on growth, and on employment. Britain began to experience mass unemployment in the late 1920s, well before the rest of the world entered the depression.

There was no ready solution to this problem of depressed British aggregate demand. Britain could not unilaterally devalue the pound, a move that would make imported goods more expensive and stimulate demand for British products. Exchange rates were set in terms of so many units of foreign currency, say the French franc, to the pound. For the pound to drop in value, the franc would have to rise. But France could always keep the franc from appreciating by selling it in large volume—and it had an endless supply of francs—in foreign exchange markets. British devaluation, in other words, could spark responsive devaluations by its trading partners. If Britain tried to support domestic demand with tariffs and other interventions, it again invited offsetting interventions by foreign governments seeking to satisfy their continuing need for sterling reserves. As Keynes tried to anticipate the postwar world in 1944, one of his chief concerns was that these kinds of competitive, beggar-thy-neighbor policies would undermine global economic growth and lead to a recurrence of the depression.

Keynes's solution to these issues was primarily to shift the role of reserve currency, with its attendant costs and benefits, from Britain to the larger, more dynamic, and less war-ravaged economy of the United States. In addition, the IMF would have access to foreign exchange reserves that could be temporarily lent to countries experiencing unusually high demands for reserve currency. He hoped that this backup insurance would reduce the overall demand for reserves and thereby shield the United States, as the principal reserve currency country, from the kind of deflationary pressures that Britain had experienced when it had that role.

The system that Keynes crafted worked remarkably well for 25 years, until around 1970. After a transition to more flexible exchange rates in the early 1970s, it continued to function for another 30 years. But then, now, the burdens that Britain experienced in the 1920s and 1930s have returned to torment the United States and the global monetary system.

Chronic Surplus Countries
and Monetary Mercantilism

Today, these basic difficulties have been worsened by a second feature of the global monetary system that Keynes also recognized in 1944 as a potential source of trouble. Some countries run international current account surpluses for reasons beyond their need to accumulate foreign currency reserves. For example, Japan has always thought of itself as a resource-poor country entirely dependent for its prosperity on favorable access to raw materials from overseas—energy, food, metals, and so on. In order to assure this access, the Japanese have striven to have their exports of manufactures to the rest of the world exceed their required imports of raw materials by a wide margin. So in addition to accumulating a large stock of foreign currency—dollar—reserves, the Japanese have also tried to maintain a continuous margin of safety in their current account balance. Except for the oil-shock years of 1975 and 1980, Japan has seen large and steadily increasing current account surpluses (Table 6.1).

Table 6.1   Japan ($ millions)

Year	Current Account Surplus
1970	2,000
1975	(690)
1980	(10,750)
1985	49,170
1990	35,870
1995	111,044
2000	119,660
2001	87,798
2002	112,447
2003	136,215
2004	172,059
2005	165,783

SOURCE: International Financial Statistics.

To maintain this surplus, they have relied primarily on two tools. First, they have restricted foreign imports, either directly by tariffs or more recently by more subtle and informal means, such as safety and other requirements that are expensive for foreign producers to meet. Anyone who has bought an orange in Tokyo has seen the impact of these policies on the prices of imported goods. Second, they have also controlled the price of yen in the international exchange markets. By keeping it low relative to foreign currencies, they have made Japanese goods cheaper in overseas markets and overseas goods more expensive in Japan. The monetary authorities can drive down the price of yen either directly by selling them in foreign exchange markets or indirectly by lowering interest rates in Japan relative to those overseas. The latter move virtually compels investors in Japan to move their assets overseas in search of higher returns and, in the process, to sell yen for foreign currencies to invest elsewhere.

China runs similar large and growing surpluses for different reasons. China's high rate of economic growth has been driven by the large and increasing volume of its exports. Domestic demand has not been sufficient to support this growth, in part because Chinese consumers save up to half of their incomes. Also, using fiscal and monetary measures to stoke domestic consumption is made difficult by the weakness of the tax collection system, which limits government spending, and by the relative disorder and lack of controls in its financial and banking system. By default, the only effective way to stimulate demand for Chinese goods is to fuel exports by keeping the value of the currency artificially low. This approach has led to chronic and growing Chinese current account surpluses, as Table 6.2 makes apparent.

European economies such as Germany have also maintained large and growing surpluses, again for reasons that are different from Japan and China. These countries have big and politically powerful manufacturing industries. The companies

Table 6.2   China ($ millions)

Year	Current Account Surplus
1980	5,823
1985	(11,417)
1990	11,878
1995	1,618
2000	20,518
2001	17,401
2002	35,422
2003	45,875
2004	68,650
2005	160,818

SOURCE: International Financial Statistics.

and the unions in concert exert an almost irresistible pressure on government policies, regardless of whether the governments are center-left or center-right politically. However, these countries face a fundamental problem. Given the broad trend toward service consumption (which we discussed in Chapter 1) and rising productivity in the manufacturing sector, employment levels and even the economic viability of manufacturing firms cannot be sustained by domestic European demand alone. To survive, these manufacturers have to export a large and growing volume of goods to the rest of the world. Sustaining these levels of net exports requires government intervention to keep the euro from rising too high against other currencies. The cries of pain as it moved from $0.90 to $1.50 and beyond in this decade illustrate the stakes. The governments also have provided more direct support for European manufacturers, as in the case of Airbus. The result is large and growing surpluses in the balance of trade for countries such as Germany, as is demonstrated in Table 6.3.[1]

Table 6.3   Germany ($ millions)

Year	Current Account Surplus	Trade Surplus
1970	850	5,690
1975	4,410	16,900
1980	(13,990)	8,056
1985	17,030	28,468
1990	48,307	68,590
1995	(19,769)	63,910
2000	(31,995)	55,464
2001	482	87,141
2002	41,049	125,755
2003	45,797	144,739
2004	101,794	187,563
2005	115,519	189,241

SOURCE: International Financial Statistics.

Still other countries, such as the oil-exporting nations, have natural surpluses with the rest of the world, which are enhanced when global prosperity and high levels of global demand drive up raw material prices. Saudi Arabia, Kuwait, and the other oil-exporting countries in the Middle East will run large current account surpluses for the foreseeable future, as global growth keeps demand for oil, and thus oil prices, high and growing.

Finally, there are countries such as South Korea, Thailand, Indonesia, Malaysia, Brazil, Mexico, and Argentina that have suffered from running current account deficits and do not want to repeat the experience. For example, South Korea has run large and increasing surpluses since the crisis of the late 1990s (Table 6.4). In keeping the value of the won depressed, restricting imports, and supporting export-oriented firms such as Samsung, South Korea has emulated Japan and maintained a current account surplus.

Table 6.4   South Korea ($ millions)

Year	Current Account Surplus
1970	(623)
1975	(1,889)
1980	(5,321)
1985	(1,745)
1990	(8,665)
1995	12,251
2000	8,033
2001	5,394
2002	11,950
2003	28,714
2004	28,174
2005	16,559

SOURCE: International Financial Statistics.

The other countries mentioned previously have implemented similar policies with the same consequences, so that they have moved as a group from deficits to chronic surpluses in their current account balances.

The "new mercantilism" of these countries has exacerbated the situation originally created by the need for reserves. It is difficult to control. As Keynes understood, deficit countries are subject to foreign pressure and control, since they need foreign currency to finance their deficits. Surplus countries are not under these constraints. They sustain their surpluses by selling their own currency, of which they have an unlimited supply, and driving down its value. In the process, they accumulate foreign currency reserves, which helps eliminate restraints on their behavior. Controlling surplus countries was a problem that Keynes did not solve at Bretton Woods.

The Global Financial System and Global Economic Stability

Considered by itself, each surplus country provides a benefit to the global economy. When the Japanese sell high-quality manufactured goods to the rest of the world in amounts that exceed by a large margin what they buy from overseas, they are like a virtuous household that produces for the benefit of others and limits its own consumption of goods produced by those others. Looked at in isolation, Germany is in the same position when it produces high-quality cars and machinery to sell abroad. So are the oil-exporting states of the Middle East, and so also are China and other Asian countries that supply a wide variety of high-quality goods at bargain prices. Without these goods, the rest of the world, including the United States, would be measurably less well-off.

The problem is that these surplus countries cannot realistically be considered one by one, in isolation from everyone else. It is the aggregate of all these surpluses that matters. The one inescapable fact of international economic life is that the sum of surpluses and deficits for all countries taken together has to equal zero. This fact is as true today as it was for Keynes in the 1930s and 1940s. If some countries are chronically in surplus, other countries must run deficits in their current account balances that, in total, are equal to the sum of the surpluses. For many years, the group of chronic deficit countries included South Korea, Indonesia, Malaysia, and Thailand. But they had to incur dollar-denominated foreign debts to finance their deficits. Over time, the continuing deficits undermined the confidence of lenders in their ability to repay. The result, as we saw in the previous chapter, was that in the late 1990s there was a run on their currencies as foreign investors tried to sell their accumulated supply of East Asian debts, and other assets. The damage to these countries was painful and traumatic. The increased burden of their foreign debts drove domestic firms out of business and led to a severe contraction of local economic activity.

This contraction did solve the balance-of-payments problem. Domestic demand fell off severely for all goods. The decline of the local currencies made foreign goods relatively more expensive, so imports dropped even more than total demand. Cheaper currencies made products from these countries more competitive in overseas markets, leading ultimately to a sharp rise in exports. The combination of the decline in imports and the rise in exports eliminated the foreign exchange deficit in these East Asian countries. But as they moved from deficit to surplus, the exports of the chronic surplus countries still had to be absorbed. Neither Japan, China, nor Germany was prepared to see their surpluses vanish just because the East Asians had been able to eliminate their particular deficits.

So, the exports of the chronic surplus countries moved on, initially to Argentina, Mexico, Brazil, and Russia. These countries soon came under the same kind of pressure as had the East Asians. They saw the value of their currencies drop and their economies contract. And, like the East Asian countries, they, too, ultimately went from deficit to surplus in their international accounts through the same path of reducing imports and increasing their now-cheaper exports.

In the end, the only country left to absorb the global surpluses was the United States, the reserve currency country of the late twentieth and early twenty-first centuries. The United States assumed the role that Britain had played from the nineteenth century until World War II. In the presence of chronic surplus countries—large and growing surpluses—and a large and growing demand for reserves, global economic stability requires that the United States run a current account deficit that is equivalently large and growing. Since U.S. overseas debts are almost all denominated in dollars, the U.S. economy does not suffer from a decline in the dollar in the same way as did the other countries discussed here. U.S. debts held abroad actually decline in value with the decline in the dollar.

There are benefits to being the country whose money is the world's reserve currency. Americans get to export low-yielding pieces of paper in exchange for real goods and services. The countries that run a surplus with the United States necessarily accumulate dollars. In theory, they can use these dollars to buy up valuable U.S. businesses and other assets, such as real estate. But, as we discussed in the previous chapter, in practice it is difficult to compete against domestic investors who have major informational advantages. The Japanese lost fortunes in the 1980s buying U.S. assets at inflated prices, and that experience is typical. Also, as the Chinese learned when they tried to buy Unocal Oil in 2005, there are substantial political barriers to entry that prevent foreign firms from buying directly into U.S. businesses. The consequence is that those accumulated dollars go largely into low-yielding U.S. government and corporate debt.

Of course, foreigners holding these dollars complain about this system. They threaten periodically to dump their accumulated dollar assets, worth trillions, which would drive down the value of the dollar even further and undermine the U.S. economy. But to date, they have never followed through, and for good reason. In order to get rid of their dollar assets, the Chinese, for example, have only two choices. For one, they can reverse the current account balance by buying more U.S. goods and services or reducing exports to the United States. This move will repatriate dollars to the United States. But the consequences for China will be dire. They would dramatically reduce demand for Chinese goods and undermine the miracle of growth. Given the high savings rate of the Chinese, it is highly unlikely that domestic consumption could fill the slack left by the falloff in exports. Since the governing promise of the Chinese ruling party—having long ago abandoned communism whether in its Marxist, Leninist, or Maoist versions—is economic growth for everyone, reducing exports to cut back on dollar holdings will put the regime itself in jeopardy and threaten social stability, which is highly prized by everyone.

The second alternative would be to buy government debt of other countries, using dollars for the purchase. The two obvious candidates are euro bonds and yen bonds. China would buy first euros and yen, and then the bonds. Now the dollar problem has been transferred to the Europeans and the Japanese. Sale of dollars for euros and for yen drive up their prices, relative to the dollar. If the Europeans were willing to let the euro appreciate to the point at which their current account balance with the United States shifted from positive to negative, then dollars would be repatriated to the United States. But were the euro to rise this much, European manufactures would be driven out of the global marketplace and Europe would certainly suffer from severe economic stagnation or even outright depression. This process is already underway. As the euro has become attractive as a reserve currency, its value has risen sharply and manufacturing exports have fallen. Enthusiasm for the euro as a reserve currency has faded.

As long as the United States is in an overall deficit position with the rest of the world, foreign holdings of dollars must increase over time. The only way to reduce global dollar holdings is for the United States to run a balance-of-payments surplus. But the only way that happens is for the rest of the world—Japan, China, South Korea, the oil exporters of the Middle East, and Europe—to move from surplus to deficit, which is exactly what they have been unwilling to do. They have been running chronic and growing current account surpluses for their own compelling reasons. So, their choice is either to accumulate growing amounts of low-yielding dollar-denominated assets, or to do an about-face on their international trade policy, stop protecting their domestic producers, become net importers, and suffer the economic and political consequences they have been working so hard to avoid. With these unpalatable alternatives, it is not surprising that the current system has been so stable, despite all the complaints about having to accept more and more dollars.

The Situation of the United States

There is a widely shared alternative view of the continuing international deficit of the United States. This is the *twin deficits* view. The idea is that American consumers save very little and, therefore, as the government runs large deficits, with spending exceeding revenues (taxes, primarily), the only way to satisfy the resulting demand for goods is through net imports. According to this position, the current account deficit is driven by U.S. behavior, not that of the rest of the world. Their surpluses are merely the consequence, not the cause, of the U.S. deficits. The argument has some logic to it. In theory, the level of the U.S. deficit depends on both American and foreign behavior. The United States could have taken steps aimed at reducing or eliminating the current account deficit—raise taxes, curtail consumption, stop traveling abroad—and has not done so, at least not aggressively enough to do the job.

The historical record strongly suggests that foreign behavior has been the more powerful factor at work. Table 6.5 presents the history of U.S. government and U.S. current

Table 6.5   U.S. Twin Deficits ($ billions)

Year	Current Account Deficit	Government Deficit
1975	(18)	53
1980	(2)	74
1985	119	212
1990	79	221
1995	113	164
1996	129	107
1997	143	22
1998	220	(54)
1999	297	(157)
2000	416	(255)
2001	386	(92)
2002	474	231
2003	531	396
2004	666	400

NOTE: Negative numbers indicate surpluses.
SOURCE: Economic Report of the President.

account deficits. The current account deficit has grown fairly steadily since the 1970s, mirroring the steadily growing surpluses of the surplus countries. The government deficit, by contrast, has grown unevenly and even turned into a substantial surplus in the late 1990s. Over the whole period, there is no close correlation between U.S. government deficits and the current account deficit. The same lack of correlation holds for other countries. As the data in Table 6.6 demonstrate, there is no evident relationship between the two. Japan, for example, has enormous current account surpluses and large government deficits. Countries with large current account deficits, like Australia, often run substantial government surpluses.

Of all the steps the United States might take to eliminate its external deficit, the automatic and natural one would be to allow a significant decline in the value of the dollar. Foreign

Table 6.6   Global Data Twin Balances, 2004 (% of GDP)

Country	Current Account Balance	Government Balance
Australia	(5.6)	0.9
Austria	(0.6)	(2.0)
Belgium	3.4	(0.1)
Britain	(2.6)	(2.9)
Canada	1.8	1.2
Denmark	(2.2)	1.8
France	(0.3)	(3.0)
Germany	3.1	(3.5)
Italy	(1.0)	(4.4)
Japan	3.6	(6.1)
Netherlands	3.5	(2.2)
Spain	(4.9)	0.5
Sweden	7.0	0.8
Switzerland	11.9	(1.0)

NOTE: Negative numbers indicate deficits.
SOURCE: International Financial Statistics.

goods and services would be more expensive for Americans and American goods cheaper for foreigners. Taken to its logical extreme, this approach should bring U.S. purchases of foreign currencies, to buy imports and for other customary uses, in line with foreign purchases of U.S. currency. When that happens, current accounts are in balance and the U.S. deficit is eliminated. This scenario underlies the logic of flexible exchange rates.

But, as we have already seen, the chronic surplus countries are not going to let this happen. They do not want to give up their surpluses, and as Keynes recognized, it is the surplus countries who are in the driver's seat. They can always keep the value of their currencies from rising by printing more and selling it in the foreign exchange markets. China and Japan have basically followed this policy, as is evident from the fact that their currencies have not appreciated in the face of large and growing current account surpluses. Only recently have the euro and the yen started substantially to rise in value against the dollar.

Any attempt by the United States to eliminate its deficit by devaluing the dollar is likely to be met by countervailing devaluations from other countries. Other measures to eliminate the deficit, like reducing economic growth or imposing barriers to trade, are also likely to be met by offsetting adjustments from other countries.

The international deficit of the United States is largely an unavoidable consequence of the role of the United States in the global monetary system. Like Britain in the late nineteenth and early twentieth centuries, it is the reserve currency country and the consumer of last resort. The deficit is not caused by the low quality of U.S. education, the competitive shortcomings of U.S. businesses, or the low savings rate in the United States. The recent record of productivity growth in the United States has been very strong both by historical standards and when measured against the performance of other major industrial economies. Yet despite this success, the current account deficit has continued to grow. Nor is any threat to the U.S. economy simply a matter of the hard work of billions of well-educated Asians. A situation in which the United States continually buys much more from Asia than it sells to it is unsustainable in a world of flexible currency exchanges. There would be a large supply of dollars seeking to buy Asian currencies to purchase Asian goods and no demand for those dollars. The sharp decline in the dollar that would follow should ultimately eliminate any Asian productivity advantage and balance the sale of U.S. dollars—needed to buy the now very cheap U.S. goods—with Asian purchases of these dollars. Any threat to employment and prosperity arises because the exchange rates have not been allowed to adjust—the value of the Asian currencies has been depressed by policy decisions—to offset the trade imbalances.

This situation gives rise to the same problem that concerned Keynes when he analyzed the experience of Britain in the first part of the twentieth century. When the United States runs a $700 billion deficit in its current account, $700 billion of U.S. purchasing power per year leaks overseas. This amounts to between 5 and 6 percent of total U.S. output and income. If the United States is to maintain full employment and high levels of output, the $700 billion must be offset by an equivalent demand for U.S. goods from other sources. In the late 1990s, the investment boom associated with the Internet bubble supplied the necessary demand. After that bubble imploded, its place was taken by a housing boom that provided the necessary demand by allowing people to spend based on the rapid rise in home prices.

But these are temporary phenomena, as we know all too well, and do not constitute a stable, long-term solution of the problem of inadequate demand for U.S.-produced goods. Generally, full-employment demand in the face of increasing trade deficits has come from a steady rise in U.S. consumer spending and an associated decline in U.S. household savings. But that trend is played out. Table 6.7 presents the course of U.S. household savings rates since the 1970s. After a steady decline, they have finally reached zero, and they are not likely to decline much further.

A continuation of increasing demand leakage overseas will inevitably translate into falling U.S. aggregate demand, stagnation of U.S. output, and rising unemployment. These are precisely the developments that Keynes saw happening in Britain, beginning in the 1920s.

Table 6.7   U.S. Savings Rate ($ billions)

Year	Disposable Income	Consumption	Savings Rate (%)
1970	736	646	9.4
1975	1,187	1,034	10.6
1980	2,009	1,757	10.0
1985	3,109	2,720	9.0
1990	4,286	3,840	7.0
1995	5,408	4,976	4.6
2000	7,194	6,739	2.3
2001	7,487	7,055	1.8
2002	7,830	7,351	2.4
2003	8,163	7,704	2.1
2004	8,682	8,212	2.0
2005	9,036	8,724	(0.4)

SOURCE: Economic Report of the President.

This situation is a problem whose impact will extend far beyond the borders of the United States. Slower growth in the United States will mean slower growth for foreign goods, and therefore slower global growth. Attempts by the U.S. government to stimulate domestic demand by reducing imports and increasing exports will, as they have in the past, be met by offsetting measures from other countries. This truly global problem is an old and familiar one, and it is not one that the United States can solve by itself.[2]

A Modest Proposal for
a New Reserve Currency

Keynes identified two fundamental problems that international monetary reform would have to solve. First, there were the inherent challenges facing any single reserve currency country.

To supply a growing world economy with the necessary reserves, the designated country would need to run large continuing deficits in its own balance of payments. But these same deficits would ultimately undermine confidence in the reserve currency. At the same time, the downward demand pressure that these deficits imposed on the reserve country's economy would reduce its long-run rate of economic growth and its relative economic position in the world. Second, chronic surplus countries imposed deflationary pressures on the rest of the world and were difficult to control. Too many countries seeking simultaneously to run international payment surpluses might force global deflation on the scale experienced during the 1930s. Though Keynes never managed to solve both problems completely, he did help create one institution, the IMF, for dealing with the first, and another institution, the World Bank, for mitigating the second.

The IMF has the potential to be a global central bank, as the Bank of England is for the United Kingdom and the Federal Reserve System is for the United States. Individual countries keep reserve accounts with the IMF, just like individual banks hold reserves with their central bank. The IMF also has a supply of currency to lend to these countries, by crediting their accounts, just as a central bank can supply money to a national economy by crediting the accounts of commercial banks. When the IMF uses this ability, it increases the global supply of reserves, just as a central bank increases the national supply of money with its credits to commercial banks. The IMF's supply of currency consists of both national currencies contributed by member countries and its own particular currency, called *special drawing rights* (SDRs), which it can create in amounts approved by its member countries. SDRs provide the IMF with the ability to create money just like national central banks can create money by printing it.[3]

In the history of the IMF, it has created SDRs intermittently and in limited amounts. But there is no reason why it could not create them regularly and in large quantities. SDRs could ultimately become the world's reserve currency, replacing the dollar or, down the road, the euro, the yen, or the yuan. Keynes certainly considered such a possibility. If the IMF were to create $200 billion to $300 billion (or 200 to 300 billion SDRs) each year, crediting the accounts of member countries in proportion to their participation in the IMF,[4] the global demand for reserves could be satisfied without the need of any reserve country to run chronic deficits. Instead, the IMF would be the deficit player. Its currency, the SDR, is valued as a weighted average of the values of all the world's national currencies. Therefore, it cannot decline unilaterally. This move would, at a stroke, solve the mandatory deficit problem of reserve currency countries such as Britain before World War II and the United States afterward.

Keynes's solution to the second problem, the deflationary pressure created by chronic surplus countries, was to stimulate offsetting levels of global demand. He hoped that one source of that demand would be the dynamism of the U.S. economy. But as well as that has worked in the past, the United States, with a zero consumer savings rate, may no longer be in a position to fulfill that role with its customary vigor. As an alternative source of global demand, Keynes looked to the investment needs of developing economies. He hoped that by lending to developing economies, the World Bank would effectively stimulate these investment demands. But, given the limitations of the effectiveness of overseas interventions, including investments in local economies, this second hope has never been realized.

However, a process of reserve creation by the IMF could be easily adopted both to stimulate global demand without detailed local interventions and to penalize the chronic surplus countries. The SDR allocations of surplus countries could be taxed at a rate proportional to their surpluses. Suppose, for example, that Japan received an allocation of 40 billion SDRs in a given year. If Japan had run a surplus of 50 billion SDRs during the prior year, then its SDR allocation would be reduced by one-half of the amount of that surplus, 25 billion SDRs. Thus, instead of receiving 40 billion SDRs, it would get only 15 billion SDRs. Such a quasi-tax, which could apply until it eliminated the whole initial allocation, would impose a cost on surplus countries such as Japan without actually taxing them directly. It could reduce the incentives for Japan to run chronic and large surpluses.

The proceeds of these virtual taxes could then be reallocated to deficit countries, which would be able to run significant current account deficits, thus adding to global demand without having to borrow overseas. This would offset the deflationary pressure that the chronic surplus countries impose on their trading partners. The countries that receive this virtual tax might be those such as South Korea, Brazil, Thailand, and Indonesia, which had run deficits before suffering the consequences of currency crises. Had these countries been able to finance their deficits out of SDR reserve allocations, without recourse to foreign borrowing, they might have continued to run deficits, and in the process, helped support global demand.

The other obvious recipients would be the poor countries of the world. Reserve allocations would represent massive amounts of unconditional aid that, even if they failed to stimulate local economic development, would raise levels of consumption and well-being in the recipient country and stimulate global demand. Looked at from one perspective, the reallocation of SDRs from surplus countries to deficit countries is a transfer from savers to spenders, in recognition of the crucial role spenders play in maintaining global demand that, left to their own devices, savers would depress and make everybody worse off.

There are certainly difficulties in implementing such changes, many of them foreseen by Keynes. The IMF has hardly established a stellar record of global economic intervention. Safeguards would have to be instituted to ensure that its own bureaucratic imperatives did not compromise its global financial mission, as they have in the past. Also, something will certainly have to be required of the recipient countries to warrant that they do not waste the funds. At a minimum, steps would need to be taken to protect against looting by corrupt regimes, which might seek to borrow against future SDR allocations and spirit those funds into private overseas accounts. These countries might also have to subscribe to common, but not needlessly intrusive, codes of acceptable international behavior, for example, to accept rigorous controls on nuclear nonproliferation.

Despite all these difficulties, some change of this sort is inevitable. With the U.S. consumer tapped out, and European industries just learning the downside of having the euro serve as a reserve currency, the status quo is clearly not sustainable. The sooner reform along these lines comes about, the better it will be for the global economy.

Conclusion

Beyond Economics

Despite all the noise on television and the campaign trail, the actual impact of globalization on our lives has not been as momentous, for good or ill, as commentators suggest. We do not discount the pain for workers who lost manufacturing jobs as production shifted overseas or the gain to consumers from lower-priced goods imported from China and other developing countries. We seek to put all those changes into perspective.

First, looking ahead, the trends point strongly to an economy in which services play a larger role. Most services are domestically produced and consumed. Over time, the world may learn to trade many more services, just as it learned to trade differentiated manufactures from the 1920s on, after global commerce had cut its teeth on raw materials and bulk commodities. But this will be a protracted process, and in the meantime, the increasing significance of services means the declining importance of globalization.

Also, economic development is due to local choices, not global conditions. As we have pointed out in some detail, economic policy at the national level changed the standard of living of hundreds of millions of Chinese, Indians, and other Asians. Globalization was part of the story, no doubt, but it hardly played the leading role. And in developed countries, the informational advantages that benefit local investment institutions continue to mean that global capital often buys high and sells low, not the best way to make a lot of money.

Jobs in the developed world are not going to disappear because of globalization. Automation has always had a greater impact on gross job losses than trade, and we have lived with automation for more than a century. New machinery has repeatedly posed a challenge to established craft workers, as the Luddites demonstrated two centuries ago. But just as Canute could not stop the tides, so entrenched craft workers and farmers have managed only to delay, not halt, the adoption of productivity-improving inventions. Economic growth would have been meager without them. That growth has historically created managerial, professional, and other white-collar jobs for the children of the displaced workers.

For companies, coping with global markets can be difficult. But they have managed to cope effectively in the past, and the evidence of recent business profitability suggests that they continue to do so. Successful strategies will be more local, in geography and product space, than global. Large global markets, with their intense levels of competition, are the destroyers of profitability, but local service markets will provide offsetting opportunities.

Financial markets are not a major exception to the idea that local knowledge helps. Global public market investment is here and will grow. But in many financial functions, local information is crucial and those activities will continue to be performed largely at the local level. When they wander far afield, as in buying securitized mortgages that have been originated and packaged elsewhere, even respected and powerful investment firms have lost billions (along with domestic firms that also should have known better).

Second, the problems of globalization have been around for at least a century, and they have not changed substantially. History remains a useful guide for us now. In particular, the central issue of global macroeconomic balance is very much what it was when people like Keynes looked at it in the 1930s and 1940s. Cheap international jet travel arrived in the 1960s. Global communications, via telephone, came earlier. The threat from Asian manufacturers was, if anything, more severe in the late 1970s and early 1980s than it is today. We should not ignore the insights of those who dealt successfully with these earlier challenges. Alarmist and anodyne prescriptions, such as learn to educate or else wither economically, based on the idea that this round of globalization is entirely unprecedented, are almost certainly misdirected.

Globalization and Everything Else

Although this book has been exclusively about economic globalization, other significant issues are clearly part of the topic. Immigration, trade in illegal drugs, the potential for worldwide epidemics like AIDS, terrorism, and perhaps most important, environmental change are all subjects with important global implications that transcend economic concerns.

A brief examination of these matters suggests that the two basic lessons we draw from our treatment of economic globalization may apply equally to these other issues. First, in most cases, local interventions may be as or more effective than coordinated global ones. Second, established, historically validated approaches will continue to provide an effective part of any solution, notwithstanding the supposedly unprecedented global nature of the problems in question.

Illegal Immigration and the Drug Trade

We group these together because they each represent cross-border movements that are violations of policy and law. Though neither has been effectively curtailed, it seems certain that no international organization or treaty is going to do much to limit the movement of people or of illegal drugs. If any useful approaches are to emerge, they will almost certainly be local in origin and in focus. For example, if either through medical treatment or a cultural-religious movement the demand for drugs were to shrink within a rich, modern country, the results would be more significant than any international agreement. The history of the advance and retreat of illegal drug use in the United States has been driven far more by changes in domestic innovations and attitudes (for example, the introduction of crack cocaine in the mid 1980s and the decline of its use a decade later) than any success in global eradication programs. Among other problems, eradication must work everywhere; otherwise production simply shifts to areas where it is less challenged. Local enforcement, education, and treatment programs need work only in the places where they are implemented.

A similar dynamic applies to illegal immigration. The sources of the migrants are legion, either directly from adjacent countries or indirectly though countries that have weak or nonexistent controls on emigration. It is far easier for any single country to track populations and their movements within their own boundaries and across their borders than to intervene throughout the globe to halt emigration at its many points of origin. Recent changes in immigration in Europe and the United States have had more to do with changes in local attitudes, especially elite attitudes, toward immigration and population control, such as the movement for national identity cards and registration with local authorities, than with global improvements in information, transportation, and the mechanics of financial remittances. Japan, Singapore, and other countries with strict controls have not experienced significant problems with unwanted immigration.

Without doubt, as we have seen in the examples of China, India, and other Asian countries, economic growth helps to keep populations at home. Economic development, as we have noted, depends far more on local than global forces.

Health and Global Epidemics

Illnesses spread as fast or faster than the people carrying them. Avian flu, SARS, AIDS, and too many other viruses, bacteria, or other germs are no respecters of borders. Global travel for people inevitably means global travel for germs. But in this case, there are established methods of control, enhanced in response to recent experiences of the AIDS epidemic. They involve global cooperation among dedicated health professionals and medical researchers that has been evolving over many years, especially since the influenza pandemic of 1918–1920 at the height of the first wave of globalization. This kind of global cooperation within a narrow and focused community has so far done well in containing potential threats likes SARS and Avian flu. The World Health Organization (WHO) has been one of the most successful examples of global cooperation. Reliance on such focused, professional communities offers a more promising approach to dealing with potential global problems than alternative schemes of broad global governance being proposed as potential solutions. It helps, of course, that interests in combating disease may be more aligned, for example, than in setting rules for international trade.

Terrorism is increasingly regarded as a global problem. From Al-Qaeda training camps in Afghanistan and Pakistan to Islamist terrorists in Indonesia to attacks in Britain, Spain, East Africa, and the World Trade Center in New York, there are undeniably global terrorist connections. However, responding to these connections with a "global war on terror" ignores the degree to which most terrorism is local in nature. The IRA, the ETA in Spain, the Tamil Tigers in Sri Lanka, the FARC in Colombia, Islamic militants in Kashmir, Kurdish nationalists in Turkey, paramilitaries in the former Yugoslavia, Shining Path guerillas in Peru, violent sects in Japan, and Timothy McVeigh in Oklahoma City were all predominantly local actors. Earlier terrorist movements in Germany, Italy, France (from former French soldiers who had fought in Algeria), Greece, and Cyprus were, despite some international connections, local movements locally handled.

Even in dealing with global terrorist organizations, local measures like strengthened cockpit doors and locks on commercial airlines, police work that disrupted Britain's second wave of bombers, and border restrictions that kept some of the 9/11 conspirators out of the United States appear to have been at least as effective as aggressive global interventions, and much less costly.

Global initiatives that have been particularly successful seem to have arisen, as in the case of the WHO, from cooperation among focused police and intelligence groups rather than from

major international initiatives. Measures to control nuclear pro-
liferation, surely among the most pressing priorities in limit-
ing the potential damage from terrorism, enjoyed a degree of
success when expert agencies were implementing a consensus
international agenda. They have fared far less well when they
have had to depend on concerted global action against recal-
citrant nations. This latter failure is due to the breakdown, following the end of the Cold War, of an underlying consensus
in the West about the nature of the threats. And that breakdown itself exposes the difficulty of relying on new initiatives
in global government and international cooperation. Effective
control of the spread of nuclear weapons appears more likely to
arise from regional cooperation along historical lines than from
broad global efforts.

The Environment

If any set of problems requires global solutions, protecting the
environment is that set. International externalities are pervasive.
Atmospheric pollution generated by any single country, from
acid raid to carbon emissions, inevitably affects other nations.
Local logging and deforestation influences global levels of
greenhouse gases. River-borne pollutants ultimately find their
way into the world's oceans. Losses of biodiversity through
local extinction of species always have potentially global consequences. The accident at Chernobyl spread radiation throughout the world. But despite the pervasive global impact of
environmental damage, there is still a strong case to be made
that local action will be more effective in initiating action than
global efforts.

To date, the record on global environmental cooperation has
been mixed. The Kyoto Accord has not been accepted by the
United States, China, India, or other large developing countries.

The nations that have begun to implement the accord in Europe and elsewhere are those for whom its provisions are the least onerous.[1] As a result, their compliance has had a relatively small impact on global warming. The prospects for improved global implementation appear limited, as individual countries hold back their commitments until others step up their efforts. The problems of global governance and coordination have not been effectively overcome, at least not so far.

There is a success story in dealing with a major global environmental problem—the effort to control and reverse the depletion of the ozone layer. In 1977, the U.S. Congress passed an amendment to the Clean Air Act that allowed the administrator of the Environmental Protection Agency to regulate any substance that he felt might damage ozone in the stratosphere. The target of this legislation was chlorofluorocarbons (CFCs), which were widely used in various industrial products and processes as coolants, solvents, and propellants. The law was enacted before there was hard proof that the CFCs were in fact depleting the ozone layer, or that ozone layer depletion was dangerous to health and the environment.

At the same time, other countries, especially Great Britain, were reluctant to go along, worrying about disrupting important industries without firm evidence that the regulations were necessary or beneficial. In the United States, important CFC producers like DuPont had been equally resistant. But under pressure from the legislation, these firms developed acceptable substitutes for CFCs. By 1987, the availability of these substitutes and a strong case for the importance of protecting the ozone layer from CFCs led to the first truly environmental accord to be signed by all the crucial countries. The Montreal Protocol on Substances That Deplete the Ozone Layer substantially reduced the use of some extremely important industrial chemicals. It set target dates for their replacement, which was a much tougher standard than had been previously applied.[2]

The Protocol was the result of initial action by a single country that led to local technology development and ultimately to an acceptable global agreement. Local action engendered a global response, not the reverse. In fact, the history of successful environmental action has been a tale of local initiatives, such as the EPA in the United States, spreading to other countries and ultimately to a global arrangement. It has not proceeded from global agreements that then control local behavior.

It seems reasonable to think that the themes of this book— the importance of local forces relative to global ones, and the value of precedents from a long history of globalization—apply as well to environmental matters, which are of recent vintage, as to other global concerns, both economic and noneconomic. For example, the Kyoto Protocal, an international treaty aimed at reducing the emission of greenhouse gases, has been a modest success at best, without the participation of the United States, China, India, and other major economies. An approach based on speeding the development of alternative energy technologies, which will depend on primarily on private investment and national governments, may prove more effective. (3) Globalization may be an important force, but it is not unprecedented and its potency should not be exaggerated.

One Last Question

An important question remains. Why, in light of compelling evidence to the contrary, has globalization become such a pervasive focus of recent public concern? Why, in other words, are so many informed and intelligent people so certain that globalization has changed the world completely? Our answer is that while the underlying importance of globalization has not grown, its appearance has altered dramatically. In the 1980s, foreign cars were imported by intermediary agencies like Toyota USA. Only rarely did car dealers and customers deal directly with foreign companies. Today, the Internet has stripped away the veil of intervening, familiar institutions. Studios distribute films directly in overseas markets. Increasingly, American retailers deal directly with Chinese manufacturers, bypassing their former suppliers, which had shifted production abroad. Nebraska Furniture Mart, for example, now has its own purchasing managers in China, rather than relying on importers. And wherever they go, they will find that Wal-Mart, Target, and even Macy's were there before them. Consumers using the Internet may even order directly from overseas suppliers.

It is not surprising, then, that a heightened sense of connection with the world overseas has emerged, even though the economic importance of the change—eliminating a level of intermediaries—may be relatively small. And there is also the point we made in the introduction, that stories and anecdotes are compelling, no matter how representative. The old adage of the local news, "if it bleeds, it leads," has as its equivalent, "the fable beats the table." We know how important good stories are in capturing attention, and we have included in this book as many as we could. But we have tried to redress the balance toward harder, more representative, and more dispositive data. There is no shortage of tables in this brief book. The story they tell is that for whatever reason, the actual impact and the novelty of the current round of globalization have been exaggerated.

Notes

Introduction: Just How Global Are We?

1. Martin Wolf, *Why Globalization Works* (New Haven: Yale University Press, 2004), p. xvii.

2. Thomas Friedman, *The World Is Flat: A Brief History of the Twenty-First Century Updated and Expanded* (New York: Farrar, Straus and Giroux, 2006); Joseph E. Stiglitz, *Globalization and Its Discontents* (New York: W.W. Norton, 2003).

Chapter 1: It May Be News, But It Isn't New

1. Norman Angell, *The Great Illusion: A Study of the Relation of Military Power in Nations to Their Economic and Social Advantage* (New York: G.P. Putnam's Sons, 1910), p. ix.

2. Thomas Friedman, *The World Is Flat*, p. 521.

3. Published as a pamphlet, "Europe's Optical Illusion," in 1909 (London: Simpkin, Marshall) and as *The Great Illusion* in 1910. In the United States, *The Great Illusion: A Study of the Relation of Military Power in Nations to Their Economic and Social Advantage* (New York: G.P. Putnam's Sons, 1910).

172 NOTES

4. International trade is the sum of exports and imports.

5. In Table 1.4, some categories, such as housing, include some man-ufactured inputs, just as other categories, such as clothing, include retail and wholesale distribution, which are services. *Statistical Abstract of the United States.*

6. Clyde Prestowitz, *Three Billion New Capitalists: The Great Shift of Wealth and Power to the East* (New York: Basic Books, 2005); Robert J. Shapiro, *Futurecast: How Superpowers, Populations, and Globalization Will Change the Way You Live and Work* (New York: St. Martin's Press, 2008).

7. For example, Friedman, *The World Is Flat*, p. 16.

8. Frank Levy and Kyoung-Hee Yu, "Offshoring Radiology Services to India, MIT Industrial Performance Center, (Cambridge, MA, 2006), and Frank Levy and Ari Goelman, "Offshoring and Radiology," in Susan Collins and Lael Brainerd, eds., "Brookings Trade Forum 2005: Offshoring White-Collar Work," revised edition (Washington: Brookings Institution Press, March 2006).

9. Telegraph.Co.UK (http://www.telegraph.co.uk/news/uknews/1567588/India-offers-hope-for-those-too-sick-to-wait.html), October 29, 2007, cites India as expecting 175,000 people to come for pro-cedures in 2007, a number it expects to grow to over 250,000 in 2008. But, for a different and perhaps more objective view, a study by McKinsey & Co. estimates that there are currently no more than 85,000 patients who travel abroad for inpatient hospital care, and that most of them are going to the United States or other developed countries for the latest available treatments. Anecdotal stories greatly exaggerate the size of the current industry and probably overesti-mate future growth, especially travel to less-developed countries to economize on the procedures. *Wall Street Journal*, May 6, 2008, "Medical Tourism Is Still Small," p. D2.

10. *Source:* U.S. Department of Education.

11. Direct conversation with general counsel of News Corp.

Chapter 2: Countries Control Their Fates

1. Margaret Lee is a pseudonym for an actual student whom Bruce Greenwald taught in the Graduate School of Journalism, Columbia University.

2. The shift to these years from the periods used earlier is because the most comprehensive historical data on global growth, produced by Angus Maddison, use these dates as breakpoints.

3. Nicholas Kristof, "The Educated Giant," *New York Times*, May 28, 2007.

4. Bruce Greenwald and Judd Kahn, *Competition Demystified: A Radically Simplified Approach to Business Strategy* (New York: Portfolio, 2005).

5. Michael van Biema and Bruce Greenwald, "Managing Our Way to Higher Service-Sector Productivity," *Harvard Business Review*, July–August 1997, pp. 87–95.

6. We acknowledge that counting pages in the Federal Register is a crude measure of regulatory intensity. The pages may be filled with discussions about proposed regulations that are never enacted. Still, we think the magnitude of the changes supports our case.

7. The negative relationship in Table 2.7 between regulatory interventions and productivity growth appears to hold also for the Clinton and G.W. Bush administrations. But this conclusion needs to be qualified. In the mid 1990s, the method for calculating productivity growth was modified substantially and new data going back seven years were produced. The relationship in Table 2.7 continued to hold prior to this revision. Under the old measurements, productivity growth in the early years of the Clinton administration, when there was a spate of new regulatory initiatives, for example, health-care reform, was actually negative. This decline was wiped out by the revision in the mid 1990s. The old and new data do not always tell the same story. Measured by the postrevision data, productivity growth has been higher under G.W. Bush than it was under Clinton. This corresponds to the generally held view that the Bush administration has been friendlier to business and less prone to aggressive regulatory interventions that require time-consuming responses by management. Still, the number of pages in the Federal Register has expanded faster during the Bush years than during the Clinton presidency. We are not certain why, but it may be that the Clinton administration pursued its regulatory agenda in the courts after Republicans took control of Congress. Still, there remains an unavoidable ambiguity about the postrevision data.

8. The experience of countries with oil or other significant natural resource endowments also speaks to the ineffectiveness of external

material aid. The revenues from these resources are similar to, but usually greater than, Marshall Plan aid. Yet the absence of any positive impact on development has been so pronounced that it is common to speak of an "oil curse" when it comes to the relationship between resource endowments and economic development.

Chapter 3: Employment Trends for Globalization 3.0

1. Peter S. Goodman, "In N.C., a Second Industrial Revolution: Biotech Surge Shows Manufacturing Still Key to U.S. Economy," *Washington Post*, September 3, 2007, p. A01.

2. China and India do have the power to prevent these offsetting exchange rate movements. But in that case, other countries have the ability to restore balance by imposing countervailing tariffs against Chinese and Indian goods and offering countervailing export subsidies. These subsidies would actually improve the efficiency of global resource allocation, by correcting the effects of currency manipulation, and the usual free-trade arguments against tariffs and subsidies do not apply here. (See Chapter 6 for a detailed discussion of these issues.)

3. David Ricardo, *On the Principles of Political Economy and Taxation*, (London: John Murray, 1817).

4. The most recent year for which detailed occupational data are available is 2005.

5. Recent improvements are almost certainly related to growth in the service sectors in these economies, not manufacturing.

6. Alan S. Blinder is a professor of economics at Princeton University and a former vice chairman of the Board of Governors of the Federal Reserve System. The estimate of 40 million vulnerable jobs is calculated from his "Fear of Offshoring," CEPS Working Paper No. 119, December 2005. In a later paper, "How Many U.S. Jobs Might Be Offshorable?" CEPS Working Paper No. 142, March 2007, Blinder estimates that between 22 and 29 million jobs have the potential to be offshored during the next several decades.

7. Real wages have not fully made up the losses of the late 1970s and early 1980s, but real compensation has. If we were to include managers and professionals in our calculations, the picture would look substantially better. The legitimate issue here is why, after growing

at 20 to 30 percent per decade prior to 1970, real wage growth suddenly fell dramatically. Part of the story may be the decline in productivity growth in those same years. But even after productivity growth revived in the late 1980s, growth in real wages did not. There were no major job losses to foreign competition, as we have shown, so the explanation is not the undermining of demand for labor by globalization. Also, the situation has improved just as globalization has become more prominent and pronounced.

Chapter 4: Can We Make Any Money?

1. The earnings data are from the Standard and Poor's web site. The price information comes from Yahoo! Finance, also on the Web.

2. BEA statistics. Bureau of Economic Analysis, National Economic Accounts, Table 1.12.

3. The European figures include depreciation and interest payments, and so are not directly comparable to the U.S. or Japanese numbers.

4. The major potential exception here for drug companies is what happens to global patents and other intellectual property protections. But this is an area where the ultimate impact of globalization—whether it will significantly weaken protection—is far from clear.

5. There is a fourth category of nongovernmental competitive advantage in addition to the three we have discussed. Informational advantages arise when an incumbent has better information about a market than potential entrants. Since they apply most frequently in financial markets, we will defer discussion of them until Chapter 5.

6. Coke and Pepsi still beat the pulp out of each other trying to win the next round of the Cola War, but that is a different issue.

7. For a more detailed discussion of competitive advantages, barriers to entry, and the strategies firms may use to protect themselves from eroding profitability, see our book, *Competition Demystified: A Radically Simplified Approach to Business Strategy* (New York: Portfolio, 2005).

Chapter 5: International Finance in a Global World

1. Or, what amounts to virtually the same thing, they sell assets, like the local telephone system, to foreign buyers.

2. The shares discussed here are those sold by already-public companies in what are sometimes called *secondary* offerings. Companies offering shares for the first time, in *initial public offerings*, are in a different position. Similarly, a company refinancing bonds that have become due is less likely to be regarded with suspicion by investors, many of whom are themselves institutions with the same financing needs.

3. Location matters within the country as well. Venture capital firms on the West Coast dominate that region, as firms on the East Coast lead in East Coast investing.

Chapter 6: A Genuine Global Economic Problem

1. Japan also uses similar direct subsidies.

2. It has been suggested that the system is also unsustainable because the United States will ultimately be unable to pay in the interest on its foreign debt. But this is almost certainly not the case. An annual current account deficit of $700–$800 billion adds that amount to the U.S. overseas debt each year. This is about 6 percent of U.S. gross domestic output. The interest rate that the United States must pay on this debt has averaged about 2 percent in real—after inflation—terms and is likely to remain low as foreigners accumulate dollars that must be invested largely in U.S. public debt. The annual recurring interest costs of financing a single year's current account deficit is 2 percent of 6 percent, or 0.12 percent of U.S. output. But that output has been growing due to productivity improvements, to say nothing of population growth, at about 2 percent per year. Thus, each year's productivity growth adds more than 15 times as much to U.S. output, in perpetuity, than that year's current account deficit adds, in perpetuity, to U.S. overseas interest payments.

   Considered as a company, U.S. income is growing and is likely to continue to grow at rates that will enable it to handle interest on its rising debt with no difficulty. Whether Americans will continue to accept increasing overseas interest payments without complaint is another, largely political, question. A large part of U.S. government and corporate debt is already in foreign hands and no one seems to notice. Where GM's or the U.S. government's interest payments ultimately go is largely opaque to the public.

3. The central banks use the money they create to buy government bonds. But the sellers of those bonds deposit the proceeds in their own banks, which, in the United States for example, redeposit them with the Federal Reserve (central bank). The resulting increase in balances at the Fed "creates" money. This high-powered money then generates a multiple expansion of bank money. To the extent that the IMF creates SDRs, it currently lends them to countries, crediting the accounts of their central banks.

4. These proportions were initially established at Bretton Woods and have been modified regularly by common consent.

Conclusion: Beyond Economics

1. In setting emission standards against historical levels, the Kyoto Accord is easiest on nations with historically low economic growth rates and often declining populations.

2. Richard Elliot Benedick, *Ozone Diplomacy: New Directions in Safeguarding the Planet*, enlarged edition, Cambridge: Harvard University Press, 1998.

3. Ted Nordhaus and Michael Shellenberger, "Scrap Kyoto: Kyoto is dead—and that's a good thing. In its place, we need massive global investment in new clean energy technology." Demovracy Journal.org, Summer, 2008, pp. 9–19.

About the Authors

BRUCE GREENWALD is the Robert Heilbrunn Professor of Asset Management and Finance at Columbia University's Graduate School of Business, where he teaches courses on value investing, the economics of strategic behavior, globalization of markets, and strategic management, of media. Described by the *New York Times* as "a guru to Wall Street's gurus," Bruce is an authority on value investing with expertise in productivity and the economics of information.

Bruce has written a number of scholarly papers and several books for wider audiences, including *Value Investing: From Graham to Buffett and Beyond*, with Judd Kahn, et al. (Wiley, 2001), and *Competition Demystified: A Radically Simplified Approach to Business Strategy*, with Judd Kahn (Portfolio, 2005).

Prior to Columbia, Bruce taught as a professor at the Harvard Business School and Wesleyan University. He was also a research economist at Bell Laboratories and, for a one-year period beginning in 1987, was the staff economist for the Presidential Task Force on Market Mechanisms (the Brady Task Force).

Bruce holds a B.S. and a Ph.D. from the Massachusetts Institute of Technology, and an M.P.A. and an M.S from Princeton University. He lives in New York City with his wife Ava Seave.

JUDD KAHN is currently the COO of Hummingbird Management, LLC, an investment advisory firm. He is the co-author with Bruce of *Value Investing* and *Competition Demystified*. Judd and Bruce were colleagues at Wesleyan University, where he taught economics and Judd taught history. Judd is the author of *Imperial San Francisco: Politics and Planning in an American City* (University of Nebraska Press, 1980). Prior to joining Hummingbird, Judd worked as a consultant and financial executive. He has a B.A. from Harvard and a Ph.D. from The University of California. He lives in New York City with his wife Anne Rogin.

Index

184 INDEX